A MIRACLE
UNDER THE
CHRISTMAS TREE

REAL STORIES OF HOPE, FAITH
AND THE TRUE GIFTS OF THE SEASON

WITHDRAWN
PRINT

JENNIFER BASYE SANDER

A MIRACLE UNDER THE CHRISTMAS TREE
ISBN-13: 978-0-373-89263-1
© 2012 by Jennifer Basye Sander

"Painted Christmas Dreams" was originally published in *Why We Ride: Writers on the Horses in Their Lives* © 2010, edited by Verna Dreisbach, Seal Press.

Sander, Jennifer Basye, 1958-
A miracle under the Christmas tree : real stories of hope, faith and the true gifts of the season / Jennifer Basye Sander.
     p. cm.
 ISBN 978-0-373-89263-1
1. Christmas—Anecdotes. I. Title.
BV45.S26 2012
 242'.335—dc23
                    2012018674

www.Harlequin.com
Printed in U.S.A.

Contents

CONTENTS

Contents

Contents

Contents

PAINTED CHRISTMAS DREAMS

DEE AMBROSE-STAHL

Deirdre woke early, just like every December 25. She tiptoed down-stairs, hoping against hope that this would be the year her dream would come true. Her parents were already awake and seated at the kitchen table; that fact alone gave the young girl pause, as they were never downstairs on Christmas morning until much later.

"Morning, sleepy head," Ben, Deirdre's father said. "'Bout time you rolled outa the hay!" When Nancy, Deirdre's mother, tried to hide her giggle behind her coffee cup, Deirdre knew something was up.

***

So began the short story—or some variation—that I wrote every year growing up. It was my dream to walk downstairs Christmas morning and find a paint horse tied outside the picture window. I, like most girls, was obsessed with horses. Usually that obsession passes like any other fad. Mine didn't. In fact, it set down roots so firm that not even marriage to a "nonhorse" man could pull them up.

Every year I wrote a similar story, "Dreaming of My Paint Horse," and gave it to my parents, hoping that they would get the hint. It seemed they never would. Every year I looked out the picture window to find an empty yard and disappointment, a vacant space where my horse ought to be.

We were never deprived as kids, far from it. But I'd have gladly relinquished every toy, every item of clothing, even every horse statue and book for that Dream Horse.

My childhood passed, as did many of my interests. Tennis? Too much work. Knitting? Knot! Horses? Now that was the constant passion in my life. I read about them, wrote about them and even joined a 4-H club that taught about them. Of course, I also dreamed about them. My own horse, though, was always out of reach.

My two older sisters each had a horse when they were younger, but in the words of my parents, "They lost interest in the horses as soon as boys came along." How was that my fault? I didn't care about boys. Boys were dumb. This was my mantra even through my teen years, until the unthinkable happened . . . I met Ron.

Ron and I came from similar working-class backgrounds and became best friends shortly after we met. Ron was perfect in every way, except that he barely knew the head from the tail of a horse. This, I thought, I could deal with. I might even teach him a thing or two. We were engaged within six weeks and married a year later. Some things you just know.

We marked our fifth anniversary, then our tenth, and then suddenly we were looking forward to our twentieth anniversary. Through all the years, my obsession with horses lived dormant— below the surface of other goings-on, but it was present nonetheless. Ron dealt with this quirk of mine the way he dealt with most things: with a quiet smile and an "oh, well" shrug of the shoulders, thinking I would get over it someday. But someday never came.

The Internet, however, did, and its information superhighway allowed me access to horses. A voyeuristic approach, I admit, but one which at least gave relief to some of my desire. I discovered a myriad of websites that listed horses for sale, and I haunted them all. I searched for paint horses, torturing myself looking at horses I knew I'd never own. Until one day in December when I found a website owned by Sealite Paint Horses in Ijamsville, Maryland. I immediately searched the Foals page. There, my pulse quickened from a minor trot of anticipation to a full-blown gallop at finding so many paint foals, from weanlings to long yearlings. I was drawn to three in particular: two yearlings and a weanling, all beautifully marked and all fillies. My heart dropped into my shoes.

On impulse, I phoned Kim Landes, the owner of Sealite, although I felt as if I were doing something illicit. We chatted for nearly an hour about horses in general and her paints in particular, and I was thrilled when she invited me to visit. I told her about the fillies that had caught my eye. She said that all three were still for sale. The news was both a blessing and a curse.

As much as I wanted to be horse shopping, Realist Ron made an excellent point when he asked, simply and softly, "How could we afford a horse?"

"So we'll just go for a drive," I said, "look at pretty horses and that's all. We'll come home right after. I promise." I knew the truth, though.

A few days later, we loaded our two corgi dogs into the back of the Jeep and began the three-hour drive to Maryland, the home of my dream. Ron has a gift for keeping me leveled, so to speak. I am impulsive; Ron is pensive. It's been this way between us since we first met. I can see how this difference may cause grief in some marriages, but for us, it created a balance.

While we drove, I chattered on about how beautiful these foals were, how much I couldn't wait until I saw them in person, how exciting it would be to raise and train a baby and how sweet a paint's disposition is. Ron nodded a lot and spoke little.

When we arrived, I was breathless, either from my incessant talking or overgrown excitement. We met Kim, her husband Chris and the Sealite gang. I felt like I'd found the Holy Grail, or like a sixteen-year-old who gets a brand new car for her birthday. All of my senses were on overload as I tried to absorb each of the dozen or more paints all at once. Then I saw her. "Oh my God, Ron! Look at her!"

Ron followed my gaze. Off beside the run-in shed stood Sky, one of the black-and-white overo fillies I had seen on Kim's website. "Wow," was all Ron could manage, and I had to agree.

Large, brown eyes looked at us from her blazed face. The side closest to us sported a white patch that nearly covered her ribs, and on her neck was what could only be described as a bleeding heart. Her four white socks were of varying lengths, but best of all, she seemed to be very well balanced in her conformation—her graceful neck tied perfectly into a powerful shoulder, and from her back came a strong hip and rear, giving her the perfect equine engine.

As we stood looking at Sky, some of the youngsters became curious about the newcomers and warily approached us. Among them was Lacy, who promptly decided that she could fit in my back pocket. I gave her a pat and told her how pretty she was, all the while keeping an eye on Sky.

"She wants things on her own terms," I whispered to Ron as I dipped my head toward Sky. "I like that."

"You do?"

"Uh huh." Without seeming too obvious, I walked over to Sky. "Hey, sweetheart," I whispered as she smelled my hand. "How are you, baby girl? Over here all by yourself. You're not antisocial, are you?"

Sky's ears flicked back and forth like an air traffic controller's paddles as she assessed me, too. I scratched her withers, a favorite itchy spot of most horses, and saw her head lower and relax. I was hooked. Sky was independent and refused to beg for a scrap of attention from us mere humans. She was not easily spooked or skittish; she just approached new situations on her own terms. This was a familiar quality, as I too tended to set and adhere to my own terms in most situations. I wanted to see how she might do on her own.

We took Sky away from her herd mates so I could watch her move in a round pen. Her tail became a flag, and her nostrils became air horns as she floated around the pen, head held high. She trotted and cantered beautifully, and her eyes spoke volumes. They were animated but not wild, a thing I loved about her. Sky was so full of joy that it was obvious this filly loved life.

I talked with Kim about Sky's price, and I could tell that Ron was not, at this moment, loving life as much as Sky. He went off with Chris for a few minutes, then casually called over to me, "I'm going to check on the corgis." That was Ron's cue to me that he wanted to go, *now*, before I did something foolish like put a deposit on this horse.

It's fair to say that Ron would never say these things aloud, but living with him all these years, I've learned how to read his nonverbal clues. But this private message between us provoked me for some reason, even though the tiny voice of reason was knocking inside my head. Usually I'm good at ignoring that voice, but I overrode it and began to talk not just price with Kim and Chris but also transport, shot records, farrier care and the myriad details concerned with a new horse purchase. Ron stayed at the Jeep during this exchange, eyeing me warily. Eventually, I bid Kim and Chris farewell with the promise to be in touch.

Ron, predictably, didn't say a word as we started our drive home. "Tell me what you're thinking," I queried.

"What I'm thinking?" he asked. "About what?"

"The weather, Ron! What do you mean 'about what?' I mean about Sky!"

"Oh, she's nice, I guess. I don't know . . ."

"Nice?! She's gorgeous!" How could he not see this?

However, that pronouncement was met with more silence. Silence that lasted many more miles until I brought it up once again. "But she's special, Ron! And I know Kim and Chris would negotiate on her price."

In typical Sensible Ron fashion, my husband pointed out what I already knew in my heart but did not want to hear: "We can't afford a horse."

I couldn't really argue with this. The purchase price of a horse—any horse—is the easiest expense to meet. Maintaining an equine for the twenty-five years or more of its life is where the economic strain comes in. Ron was right, as he usually is in all economic matters. We could not afford a horse, period. I tempered this acceptance by adding silently, "Not now, anyway. I'll take the coward's way out and e-mail, rather than call, Kim tomorrow to tell her." These last words caught in my throat.

Later that evening, we stopped for dinner along the interstate. I don't know if it was the holiday decor of the restaurant or the Christmas section of the attached gift shop, but suddenly I was transported back in time. *It's Christmas morning. I race down the stairs and offer the brightly lit tree only a quick glance, for just past the tree is the picture window. It can't be! I shake my head and rub my eyes, certain that my mind is playing tricks on me. I look again, and it—she—is still standing there. Sky is standing in the front yard of my childhood home, her glistening black-and-white coat a stark contrast to the glimmering white Christmas snow.*

My husband's voice brought me back to reality.

"What? I'm sorry, what did you say?" I asked.

"I asked what you were thinking about. You've been really quiet, but you smiled just now," Ron said. That's when I realized that in nearly twenty years of marriage, I had never shared the story of The Dream Horse with him. Over dinner, I recounted the tale, with a bit of sadness in my voice that I just couldn't hide. Ron's normally brilliant blue eyes clouded over.

"I know exactly what you mean," he said with a sigh as he reached across the table for my hand. Like me, my husband grew up in a blue-collar family with never quite enough money. He, too, knew firsthand the feeling of The Dream, but his dream was a motorcycle on two wheels, not four hooves—the iron horse.

The rest of the drive home, we remained silent, arriving home just after dark. Exhausted and disappointed, I climbed into a hot shower and then managed to read a few chapters of a book. I fell asleep imagining my beautiful new filly cantering across the field to greet me. She offered me her soft, pink muzzle, and I wrapped my arms around her glistening neck and buried my face in her mane, breathing in her heady smell. I felt the level of contentment I'd been searching for, but it was only a dream.

***

"Are you going Christmas shopping with me on Saturday?" I asked Ron. It was December 18, and we had yet to do any big shopping for family and friends. With our work schedules, the coming Saturday was looking like our one and only hope of accomplishing any shopping together.

"Oh, um, well . . . " Ron stammered. "We can't go anywhere Saturday."

"What do you mean we can't go anywhere? We've got tons of shopping to do!"

"Well, I'm expecting a delivery, and we have to be here when it comes. You know how FedEx can be," he said.

I was furious with him for having waited until the last minute to buy my Christmas gift. Fine. I left him to his FedEx worries and did the shopping myself during the week. I was not at all gracious about this scenario.

I barely spoke to him that week, and when I did speak, it was only in short, clipped answers to something he said first. My Christmas spirit was obviously going to be absent in the Stahl home this year. I made sure this fact was not lost on Ron.

Saturday morning, I was in the den wrapping presents. I had a perfect view of the driveway via the picture window. I would certainly see the FedEx truck when it arrived.

My anger with Ron collided full force with my eagerness to catch a glimpse of the delivery. Eagerness was winning out. Where could he have been shopping? Did he go on his lunch break from work? That would limit the possibilities. Would the shipping box offer any clues? Would I know what it is from the box that it's in? Damn!

I wasn't paying attention and cut the wrapping paper too short. As I reached for a new roll of paper, Ron's thundering feet on the stairs made me jump. What startled me even more, though, was his voice. "He's here!" Ron shrieked, hitting a pitch

I hadn't heard from him in all our twenty years together. I had no idea that Ron loved the FedEx guy this much.

"Come here, come here, come here!" Ron chattered. "You've gotta come here . . ." and he pulled me by the hand to stand in the doorway facing the driveway.

"Look!"

And then I did, but what I saw didn't register. White SUV. SUV? Pulling something. A horse trailer. A horse trailer? A horse trailer with "Sealite Paint Horses" written on the side!

I staggered backward, into Ron's arms, and he kissed me on the head as he draped a coat over my shoulders. "Let's go," he whispered in my ear, gently pushing me out the door.

As my brain spun circles trying to wrap itself around this image, the driver's window of the SUV rolled down, and the vehicle rolled to a stop. "Merry Christmas, Dee!" I heard the driver yell—wait, that's Chris!

I remember Chris getting out of the vehicle and giving me a hug. I remember holding my breath as he dropped down the window of the trailer. And I remember thinking, *She's home*, as her familiar white face popped out from behind the window. She looked at me, and her soft brown eyes reflected, "I remember you."

As I stroked her beautiful white face, I said something brilliant to Chris like, "You were supposed to be the FedEx guy!"

So how did Ron do it? How did he make my dream come true?

Apparently, the night we returned from Sealite, he called Kim and Chris and made the arrangements, all on the sly. My sad story of yearning and Christmas disappointment had moved him to action.

I stood wrapped in Ron's arms, watching Sky become acquainted with her new home. I turned and looked into Ron's eyes. My question was simple: "Why?"

"Because you wanted her from the beginning. I wanted to be the one who made your dreams come true."

Somewhere, in the deep, dark recesses of my memory, I felt the curtain drop down on an old yearning and a new kind of contentment fill every bit of those years of wanting and waiting. Then, I felt another curtain rise above a thousand new dreams as I settled my head against Ron's chest and looked into the eyes of my new paint dream.

Ron and I smiled, laughed, cried tears of joy and talked well past midnight about our new dreams and how we might make them come true for each other.

CALIFORNIA CAMPER CHRISTMAS

CHERYL RIVENESS

It was Christmas morning 1986. Thinking back to the day before, I recalled how everything had come together. It had been a pretty bad year, and Christmas promised to be more of the same. A fabulous holiday for the children was a luxury we couldn't afford. I had all but given up hope that we would be able to celebrate even in a small way. And then, my husband, a truck tire service technician, received an unanticipated service call. The driver was stranded and trying desperately to make it home in time to be with his own children on Christmas morning. He was short of money, but he had merchandise that he was willing to trade for services, enabling us to give the older girls, eleven and thirteen, exactly what they'd wanted: a VCR.

Two days before, we had driven sixty-five miles to pick up the one thing that our youngest had asked for (a Disney Fievel plush toy) before closing time. The drive and the toy had taken everything we had saved. I scoured pockets and the truck seat on the morning of Christmas Eve and found just over three dollars in change. Feeling optimistic, I headed for the nearest flea market, arriving just as the vendors were packing up.

I had tried repeatedly to get the kids to understand that there simply wasn't enough room for a tree in the dilapidated pickup camper that the five of us had been calling home for months now. But, I thought, maybe a string of lights and little candy canes would make the surroundings more festive. The camper was small, so luckily one string would do. As I was paying the vendor, something caught my eye, a glimpse of a very small, white artificial tree top being tossed from row to row by the breeze. Hastily wishing the old gentleman a merry Christmas, I waved goodbye and rushed after the treasure. My heart absolutely swelled with appreciation. Now I could grant their special wish, if only in a small way.

That evening, after we'd watched *Frosty the Snowman* and enjoyed popcorn and hot chocolate, I tucked the children in and listened to their prayers. They were simple: "Please help us find a home soon." I couldn't help thinking how Joseph and Mary must have been feeling the night of Jesus's birth; they too were homeless. At least we had shelter.

Once the girls' breathing was soft and measured, I retrieved the lights and the tree from inside the truck cab, and after quietly weaving the lights around the small branches, I asked my husband to place the tree in the corner above our youngest child's bed. After he managed to safely tuck it in, he ran the string down the length of the overhead cabinets and to the electrical outlet. "Well, here goes nothing," he mouthed, plugging the cord into the socket. We held our breath and waited. They came on, and they twinkled, with the smallest blue lights, their reflection glinting off the rusted chrome trim of the tiny "kitchen."

The night had been cold, the steady wind magnifying the plummeting temperatures. Assorted leaves and debris still blew through the campground, and our large dog was crying to get inside. I was drained, mentally and emotionally. Crawling into our bunk, I pulled the curtain closed behind me; the gentle blue glow of the lights dancing on the ceiling lulled me into satisfied slumber.

Waking to hushed whispers, I heard Arianna's voice, quiet in the early light of dawn: "Santa brought us a tree! Look, Sissy, it's so pretty, and it's ours." Peaking through the curtains, I saw that our min pin dog was still nestled asleep in her arms, his breathing rhythmic. Her eyes were fixated on the little tree that had appeared while she slept.

I lowered myself from the overhead bunk onto the burnt orange cushion of the seat below. "Oh, Mommy, it's so beautiful," she whispered in amazement. "I didn't even *hear* him," she continued with the wide-eyed wonder that only four-year-olds possess. Santa had brought both of the things she had wanted so much. The little white tree top was absolutely resplendent, and her toy was a treasure that she still has thirty-some years later.

It would be several years before our Christmases became more like the ones the older girls remembered. Yet, when we speak of childhood memories, the magic of this special morning is among our favorites.

CHRISTMAS LOVE

CANDY CHAND

This story shows up every holiday season in e-mail inboxes around the world, frequently attributed to Anonymous. But it is not from an anonymous writer; it is a real-life experience from my friend Candy Chand. I had the privilege of publishing Candy's first story ever in my book *The Magic of Christmas Miracles,* and she hasn't stopped writing since. You will be as touched as the millions who have read this.

—*Jennifer Basye Sander*

Each December, I vowed to make Christmas a calm and peaceful experience. But once again, despite my plans, chaos prevailed. I had cut back on nonessential obligations: extensive card writing, endless baking, decorating and, yes, even the all-American pastime, overspending. Yet, still, I found myself exhausted, unable to appreciate the precious family moments and, of course, the true meaning of Christmas.

My son, Nicholas, was in kindergarten that year. It was an exciting season for a six-year-old filled with hopes, dreams and laughter. For weeks, he'd been memorizing songs for his school's winter pageant. I didn't have the heart to tell him I'd be working the night of the production.

Unwilling to miss his shining moment, I spoke with his teacher. She assured me that there'd be a dress rehearsal the morning of the presentation. All parents unable to attend that evening were welcome to come to the dress rehearsal. Fortunately, Nicholas seemed happy with the compromise.

So, just as I promised, on the morning of the dress rehearsal, I filed in ten minutes early, found a spot on the cafeteria floor and sat down. Around the room, I saw several other parents quietly scampering to their seats. As I waited, the students were led into the room. Each class, accompanied by their teacher, sat cross-legged on the floor. Then, each group, one by one, rose to perform their song.

Because the public school system had long stopped referring to the holiday as Christmas, I didn't expect anything other than fun, commercial entertainment: songs of reindeer, Santa Claus, snowflakes and good cheer. The melodies were fun, cute and lighthearted, but nowhere to be found was even the hint of an innocent babe, a manger or Christ's sacred gift of hope and joy. So, when my son's class rose to sing "Christmas Love," I was slightly taken aback by its bold title.

Nicholas was aglow, as were all of his classmates, who were adorned in fuzzy mittens, red sweaters and bright wool snow-caps. Those in the front row—center stage—held up large letters, one by one, to spell out the title of the song. As the class sang, "C is for Christmas," a child held up the letter C. Then, "H is for happy," and on and on, until they had presented the complete message, "Christmas Love."

The performance was going smoothly, until suddenly, we noticed her: a small, quiet girl in the front row who was holding the letter M upside down. She was entirely unaware that reversed, her letter M appeared to be a W. Fidgeting from side to side, she soon moved entirely away from her mark, adding a gap in the children's tidy lineup.

The audience of first through sixth graders snickered at the little one's mistake.

But in her innocence, she had no idea that they were laughing at her as she stood tall, proudly holding her "W."

One can only imagine the difficulty in calming an audience of young, giggling students. Although many teachers tried to shush the children, the laughter continued until the last letter was raised, and we all saw it together. A hush came over the audience, and eyes began to widen.

In that instant, we understood—the reason we were there, why we celebrated the holiday in the first place, why even in the chaos there was a purpose for our festivities. For when the last letter was held high, the message read loud and clear:

CHRIST WAS LOVE

And I believe He still is.

UNFINISHED GIFTS

BJ HOLLACE

"I need to find the perfect gift. I need to find the perfect gift." The words circulated through my mind like the woodpecker that tapped on our chimney. Christmas was coming, and I needed it to be perfect this year.

Years had passed since my entire family had celebrated together around one Christmas tree. Those things that had kept us apart, including time and distance, were being put aside. It was time to heal old wounds. Forgiveness and healing were on my Christmas list this year.

The search began for the perfect gift for my mother. What does a perfect gift look like anyway? My mom's favorite treats are Brown & Haley's Mountain bars, so I quickly scribbled those onto the list. Hmmm, what else? The blank page stared back at me. Candy, even her favorite candy, was not going to be sufficient.

"What can we get for my mom?" I asked my husband, Bill. He shrugged his shoulders. Clearly, this assignment would require some soul-searching. Sometimes even husbands don't have all the answers.

As I went about my daily tasks, I thought and prayed and thought some more. Suddenly, in my mind, I could see the perfect present in wonderful detail. I knew exactly what would surprise and delight my mother, but the question was, Where was it? Living in a one-bedroom apartment, my filing system isn't what you would call perfect. It is adequate for those things that are filed, but as for the unfiled items stored in miscellaneous bins, well, it would be like finding a needle in a haystack.

Somewhere in the apartment was a gray envelope sent by my brother and sister-in-law about a year earlier. Inside were several photos and a note from my mom. I walked from room to room, eyeing stacks and piles. *Which one had I put it in?* After some digging, I found it. The first piece of the puzzle was in my hand. As I opened the envelope, I found the photos and note just as I remembered.

My great-grandmother Janke liked to knit. As a family tradition, she'd made baby bootees for her grandchildren and great-grandchildren. The photos showed an unfinished bootee with knitting needles still stuck in it, as if she'd put it aside for a few moments to go make a cup of tea.

My mom's request was that I write a short poem to go with this photo. I was touched and flattered that she'd asked, of course, but then reality set in. I didn't have a clue how to put words to this piece of my history. How can you honor someone who died when you were only two years old? I never really knew her, not like my mom knew her grandmother.

Memories of my own grandma and the many hours I spent with her over a cup of tea or laughing, baking and praying came easily to mind. Grandma is long gone. She was my mother's mother—she is a part of me.

I had the photo, now I needed some inspiration. Maybe if I knew more about the actual woman, I could give her the tribute she deserved. Hmmm, I looked around my apartment again, checking all the logical places for the family history book. Ah, yes, here were the facts. Janke Heeringa was born on January 22, 1874, in Holland. In May 1891, seventeen-year-old Janke came to America by herself, joining her brother and sister who lived in Iowa. Immediately, she began doing household work in the area for American people even though she knew no English. She was married two years later in 1893 to my great-grandfather.

In October 1900, twenty-eight Hollanders from Iowa rented a train car and hired a porter to help them travel to Washington to start a new life. When Janke began the journey from Iowa, she was seven months pregnant and had three young children, all boys—two, four and six years old—to care for as well. Her fourth child was born in December 1900 after arriving in the Pacific Northwest.

Janke was described as a woman of determination. *Yes, you would have to be to survive that cross-country trip while pregnant*, I thought. *My mother and grandmother and even I could be described that way.* Must be a family trait.

When Janke died in 1961 at the age of eighty-seven, she left behind twenty-five grandchildren, fifty-six great-grandchildren and one great-great-granddaughter. Great to have so many solid facts, but I was still without a shred of poetry.

The clock ticked on. This present didn't need to be finished until we arrived to visit family just after Christmas, but time was still short. The days flew by as I struggled to find the right words. How could a poem and picture convey the message of healing and forgiveness that I sought? Only God knew. I still didn't get it.

My husband and I talked again. "It's something that I need to do. The time is right, but I just don't know what to say."

"I know you can do it. I have faith in you."

"Thanks, sweetheart. It's more than faith I need. I need divine inspiration."

Finally, I was at peace. My struggle for understanding was over. Mentally and emotionally, I stood in her shoes, this woman who was part of me, whose blood ran through my veins. The answer was etched in my DNA. I just needed to write what was in my heart.

The frame was small, so the poem needed to be Goldilocks size—not too long and not too short, just right.

I needed to understand the subject matter, my great-grandmother, but also the audience, my mother. Mom had a special relationship with her grandmother. I understood that kind of grandmother–granddaughter relationship. For inspiration, I drew on the stories Mom shared of visiting Janke on Saturday afternoons after catechism and again on Sundays after church, sitting on her grandma's lap and slurping tea from the saucer. And if she was really good, dried apples were a special treat.

How could I bring these generations of women together? My great-grandmother and grandmother had passed on to their heavenly reward, leaving my mom navigating through life's changes, and me, who hoped to unite these generations with words and give them the honor they deserved.

I needed my poem to be a mixture of love, healing and wholeness that we seek to find in our families. It was a high calling, but I knew it was possible. Finally, the words came. The message was short, laden with emotion, and it painted the picture I saw in my mind—to honor Janke and this moment.

Holding the paper before me, I read it out loud in its final form and knew this was it.

With each stitch, she weaves a prayer,
for the tiny foot that will fit in there.
She stops for a moment and gazes outside;
the children are looking for a place to hide.
Her trembling hands slow her pace;
she knows that soon she'll see her Savior's face.
Now her knitting needles lay silent . . .

Yes, it was right. I believed it conveyed the message on my great-grandmother's heart in her final days. She knew the time had come to go to her husband, gone almost twenty years previously. Janke was ready, ready enough to leave this last bootee unfinished.

The photo and poem were carefully framed and secured in my carry-on bag as we flew across the state. The gift was precious and couldn't be trusted as checked baggage to be jostled around in the plane's belly. It wouldn't leave my sight until it was delivered to its intended destination.

We all gathered for Christmas at my parents' home, a place laden with memories. The Christmas tree was surrounded by mountains of gifts, and Mom's special package was tucked safely in a corner.

When it was Mom's turn, she opened several gifts before opening ours. Tearing away the paper, Mom realized quickly what it was, gasping as she removed the last scrap of wrapping. A piece of her grandma Janke was returned to her that day.

Four generations of women were united that night. We were four women who had known life's joys and sorrows. Women who were filled with determination to live their lives with all they had and to offer no less than the best to their families and their Creator. Women who know that miracles are found every day in unusual places, not just in perfection but also in the unfinished projects of our lives. There are miracles in the making that are often left for future generations to piece together until the circle is complete. My part was finished. I closed the circle of love that Janke, my great grandmother, set in motion years ago while traveling from her birth country to a land she did not know, a land where she would find hope and love and, yes, miracles.

DICKENS IN THE DARK

JENNIFER ALDRICH

It seemed like a good idea at the time. *"Come to the Great Dickens Christmas Fair with me," he had said. "You will be able to dress in a beautiful costume."* And here I stood, in a plain, twill, button-down dress, watching the rain pounding the steel roof, the sound louder on the inside than outside. How did I get here?

Daniel, my husband of three months at that point, and I were spending our Christmas season working at the largest Dickensian festival in California. San Francisco's Cow Palace becomes London as Dickens saw it for four or five weekends each year.

Charles Dickens's characters are here: all the ones you would expect for this time of year (Mr. Scrooge and Tiny Tim) and others you may not expect to see at Christmas (Mr. Fagin and Bill Sikes), not to mention Mr. Charles Dickens himself. In addition to the Dickens characters, there are historical characters of the

Victorian Era (Queen Victoria and Prince Albert) and even some fictional characters known to all at the time (Father Christmas, Sherlock Holmes and Mr. Punch).

Rounding out this eclectic collection of characters is the family of Charles Dickens himself. That's where we are: the Dickens's Family Parlour. Daniel is Charley Dickens, the eldest and most ne'er-do-well of Dickens's seven sons. I am Mrs. Cooper, the cook. I make a midday meal to feed the actors in our immediate cast of twelve.

It was the last day of the Fair for the season, and I had been inside the building since 8 a.m. preparing a special tea for singing performers, getting water hot before everyone else arrived. By 10 a.m., my castmates were dressing in our environmental area, the carpeted Parlour floor a sea of hoopskirts and crinolines. We all dress in costumes appropriate to the period, with great care given to historical accuracy. As I was playing a servant, I did not have the hoops under my skirts that the other ladies of my household were wearing. But like them, I was in a laced-up corset, long dress and button-up boots; my pin bib apron and hair tucked under a mop cap completed my less than glamorous look.

"I'm going to deliver teas now," I said to Mamie, the eldest Dickens daughter and our director. "I'll be back before opening."

"You okay, honey?" she asked concerned. "You look done."

"Stick a fork in me," I replied. "I'm just glad it's the last day of the season."

In truth, I was exhausted. There are some things which, even though you love to do them, can take a lot of effort. Working at the Dickens Fair was a lot of work, plus I had a full-time job on the weekdays. Also, it can be a very expensive hobby. This was the first year I worked at the Fair. I had only attended once before as a patron, watching Daniel perform in one of the stage shows.

I have always loved the fantasy of time travel and have been an avid reader of historical novels for years. I had such a great time as a patron that I decided to join in, jumping into the deep end feet first. I could be, if only for a short time, somewhere and someone else, to live the fantasy. I could have asked to do something simpler to start, but I have a hard time asking for help, especially when it involves doing something I say I like doing.

I walked out of the Parlour, near the entrance to the Fair, past the stalls and storefronts of the artisans who sell their wares of Christmas decorations, bonnets and wreaths, pewter goblets and jewelry. I headed into the breezeway, home of the London docks and the Paddy West School of Seamanship, which is in reality a band of very musical sailors who sing sea chanteys and nautical songs. I dropped off one air pot of tea, received a hug of thanks from one of the cabin "boys"(a lively woman with short hair) and headed down to Mad Sal's Dockside Alehouse at the other end of the bay to drop off the rest. Mad Sal's is where naughty music hall songs are performed and represents the seedy end of our London.

The rain was really coming down, booming and loud against the roof, the occasional thunderclap joining in for good measure. Heading backstage, I dropped off the last air pots to Weasel, our chief chucker in the Music Hall. Short in stature but big in heart, he can get you to sing along with a music hall ditty faster than you can say "Burlington Bertie from Bow."

"Oy! Weasel!" I said, in my best Cockney accent. "Where's Sal an' everybody?"

"Over by the door," he replied, gesturing with his thumb. "I'm stayin' in 'ere. Too bleedin' cold for me near the door."

"Too right," I said, nodding at the air pots. "I'll pick 'em up afore the last show."

I turned away from the stage and headed back to the Parlour along the sidewall of the Concourse. I saw Mad Sal, Dr. Boddy, Molly Twitch, Polly Amory and a few others sitting and watching the rain. I gave a quick wave and continued walking.

"Gee," I heard someone say, "you think all this rain might affect attendance?"

Suddenly, there was another loud thunderclap, and POP all the lights went out! The few exit lights in the building came on immediately after.

"That might," came the reply.

We will not be opening the Fair on time today, I realized. The entire hall felt nearly pitch-black at first, with the exception of the exit signs. We wouldn't be able to bring customers in until we could get the lights back on. I slowly made my way back to the Parlour, taking my time and stepping carefully, overhearing pieces of conversations as I went.

"Somebody forgot to pay the electric bill!"

At an ale stand: "I guess we have to drink all the champagne before it gets warm."

Someone talking to the dancing light of a cell phone screen: "What's that, Tink? The pirates have captured Wendy?"

I came back into the Paddy West area to see the whole group sitting on the stage, playing softly in the semidarkness. The side exit doors had been opened a crack to let in some light. I didn't want to move another step back into the darkness of the next bay, so I sat down on one of the benches facing the stage.

They started to play my favorite sea chanty, "Rolling Home." The beauty of the music, my fatigue, the dark and the rain all came together and washed over me. I started to cry. Then I started to think.

Do I really want to do this, year after year? "Rolling home, rolling home." *I am so wiped out, and it's such a huge commitment.* "Rolling home across the sea." *Is this something that Daniel and I should share?* "Rolling home to dear old England."

What if we have kids? Will we bring them, too? "Rolling home, fair land to thee."

Our minutes in the dark stretched on past 11 a.m., our opening time. I returned to the Parlour at about 10:45. Daniel and I began to take the small, unlit candles off our Christmas tree, light them and set them in candelabras on the dining table. It gave a beautiful glow to our set, now a very realistic looking Victorian parlor.

We sat down at the settee, and I told him about my little breakdown in the Paddy West area. He held my hand and said, "Okay, today is our last day."

"Yeah," I said, "until next year."

"No," he said, "our last day ever. I don't want you to do anything that doesn't make you happy. And I definitely won't make you do something that is supposed to be just for fun when you hate it."

It didn't sound right to me the minute he said it. *I love doing this,* I thought. *I love creating the type of Christmas that probably never existed, but we all wish could have. I love the friends I've made here. They've become my family.*

"I love you," I said finally. "I love that you would be okay with my quitting. But I'm not going to. I found my people, where I belong. I may do things a little different next year to make it easier, but I won't give it up. There would be too many things I would miss and too much."

Daniel smiled at me in a way that told me he had known I would change my mind, cheeky bugger. Before we met, I wrote down all the things I wanted in a guy. One of them was "someone who would call me on my nonsense." Damn if I didn't find him.

A call went out to the cast members inside to gather together all the umbrellas in the building; the line of customers had extended past the building well into the parking lot for several yards. Charles Dickens and other cast members went out to hold the umbrellas and keep everyone as dry as possible. All the musicians available entertained them. The servers from Cuthbert's Tea Shoppe came out, too, dispensing hot tea.

Some people were escorted in small groups past the Parlour to the restrooms. Walking past, one woman gave a small gasp. "Oh!" she said, turning toward the Parlour and seeing our candlelit set, "You all look like a painting!"

By 11:30, I was providing the last of our tea supply to Cuthbert's when the lights came back on. We could hear the cheer from the crowd outside as plain as if they were standing next to us. As soon as it was safe to do so, the doors were opened to let the patrons into the Fair.

The abbreviated schedule didn't seem to diminish the experience of the day for anyone. The spirit of Christmas, it seemed, was present everywhere. Everyone was happy and smiling, patron and participant alike. The small kindnesses that our cast and crew gave to those outside was repaid tenfold back to us, in every heartfelt "Merry Christmas" and word of thanks. Patrons who had originally planned to spend only an hour or two at our fair told me they were going to stay all day, just to support us!

"Thank you for bringing the Dickens Fair outside!" one woman exclaimed.

***

That was my first year working at the Great Dickens Christmas Fair. Did I go back? Yes, and with a renewed enthusiasm. Last year, we brought our four-year-old for his first year as a participant. Daniel built a train for him out of cardboard boxes so he could be part of the Toy Parade. Bringing a baby or a small child to the Fair as a participant takes a considerable amount of careful planning, but it can be done. Those who are the most successful are those who ask for help. The Fair's community, like any large family, takes care of its own.

Will our son share our passion for this and join us even when he is older? It's hard to say at this point, but he will be raised knowing how much we love it and hearing stories of the Fairs of Christmas Past. And I am sure we will tell him about the day the Fair went dark.

***

Looking back, the best part of that day for me was seeing the quality of people in our Fair family. Some say we are crazy to spend our time, our money and our holiday season on this theatrical enterprise. But now I can't imagine a better way to spend my Decembers than with this group I am proud to work with and proud to know.

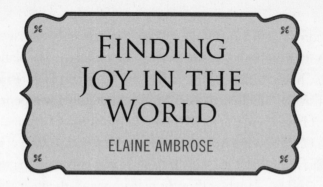

FINDING JOY IN THE WORLD

ELAINE AMBROSE

December 1980 arrived in a gray cloud of disappointment as I became the involuntary star in my own soap opera, a hapless heroine who faced the camera at the end of each day and asked, "Why?" as the scene faded to black. Short of being tied to a railroad track in the path of an oncoming train, I found myself in an equally dire situation, wondering how my life turned into such a calamity of sorry events. I was unemployed and had a two-year-old daughter, a six-week-old son, an unemployed husband who left the state looking for work and a broken furnace with no money to fix it. To compound the issues, I lived in the same small Idaho town as my wealthy parents, and they refused to help. This scenario was more like *The Grapes of Wrath* than *The Sound of Music*.

After getting the children to bed, I would sit alone in my rocking chair and wonder what went wrong. I thought I had followed the correct path by getting a college degree before marriage and then working four years before having children. My plan was to stay home with two children for five years and then return to a satisfying, lucrative career. But, no, suddenly I was poor and didn't have money to feed the kids or buy them Christmas presents. I didn't even have enough money for a cheap bottle of wine. At least I was breast-feeding the baby, so that cut down on grocery bills. And my daughter thought macaroni and cheese was what everyone had every night for dinner. Sometimes I would add a wiggly gelatin concoction, and she would squeal with delight. Toddlers don't know or care if Mommy earned Phi Beta Kappa scholastic honors in college. They just want to squish Jell-O through their teeth.

The course of events that led to that December unfolded like a fateful temptation. I was twenty-six years old in 1978 and energetically working as an assistant director for the University of Utah in Salt Lake City. My husband had a professional job in an advertising agency, and we owned a modest but new home. After our daughter was born, we decided to move to my hometown of Wendell, Idaho, population 1,200, to help my father with his businesses. He owned about thirty thousand acres of land, one thousand head of cattle and more than fifty 18-wheel diesel trucks. He had earned his vast fortune on his own, and his philosophy of life was to work hard and die, a goal he achieved at the young age of sixty.

In hindsight, by moving back home, I was probably trying to establish the warm relationship with my father that I had always wanted. I should have known better. My father was not into relationships, and even though he was incredibly successful in business, life at home was painfully cold. His home, inspired by the designs of Frank Lloyd Wright, was his castle. The semi-circular structure was built of rock and cement and perched on a hill overlooking rolling acres of crops. My father controlled the furnishings and artwork. Just inside the front door hung a huge metal shield adorned with sharp swords. An Indian buckskin shield and arrows were on another wall. In the corner, a fierce wooden warrior held a long spear, ever ready to strike. A metal breastplate hung over the fireplace, and four wooden, naked aborigine busts perched on the stereo cabinet. The floors were polished cement, and the bathrooms had purple toilets. I grew up thinking this decor was normal.

I remember the first time I entered my friend's home and gasped out loud at the sight of matching furniture, floral wallpaper, delicate vases full of fresh flowers and walls plastered with family photographs, pastoral scenes and framed Norman Rockwell prints. On the rare occasions that I was allowed to sleep over at a friend's house, I couldn't believe that the family woke up calmly and gathered together to have a pleasant breakfast. At my childhood home, my father would put on John Philip Sousa march records at 6:00 a.m., turn up the volume and go up and down the hallway knocking on our bedroom doors calling, "Hustle. Hustle. Get up! Time is money!" Then my brothers and I would hurry out of bed, pull on work clothes and get outside to do our assigned farm chores. As I moved sprinkler pipe or hoed beets or pulled weeds in the potato fields, I often reflected on my friends who were gathered at their breakfast tables, smiling over plates of pancakes and bacon. I knew at a young age that my home life was not normal.

After moving back to the village of Wendell, life went from an adventure to tolerable and then tumbled into a scene out of *On the Waterfront*. As I watched my career hopes fade away under the stressful burden of survival, I often thought of my single, childless friends who were blazing trails and breaking glass ceilings as women earned better professional jobs. Adopting my favorite Marlon Brando accent, I would raise my fists and declare, "I coulda been a contender! I coulda been somebody, instead of a bum, which is what I am."

There were momentary lapses in sanity when I wondered if I should have been more like my mother. I grew up watching her dutifully scurry around as she desperately tried to serve and obey. My father demanded a hot dinner on the table every night, even though the time he would come home could vary by as much as three hours. My mother would add milk to the gravy, cover the meat with tin foil (which she later washed and reused) and admonish her children to be patient. "Your father works so hard," she would say. "We will wait for him." I opted not to emulate most of her habits. She fit the role of her time, and I still admire her goodness.

My husband worked for my father, and we lived out in the country in one of my father's houses. One afternoon in August of 1980, they got into a verbal fight, and my dad fired my husband. I was pregnant with our second child. We were instructed to move, so we found a tiny house in town, and then my husband left to look for work because jobs weren't all that plentiful in Wendell. Our son was born in October, weighing in at a healthy eleven pounds. The next month, we scraped together enough money to buy a turkey breast for Thanksgiving. By December, our meager savings were gone, and we had no income.

I was determined to celebrate Christmas. We found a scraggly tree and decorated it with handmade ornaments. My daughter and I made cookies and sang songs. I copied photographs of the kids in their pajamas and made calendars as gifts. This was before personal computers, so I drew the calendar pages, stapled them to cardboard covered with fabric and glued red rickrack around the edges. It was all I had to give to those on my short gift list.

Just as my personal soap opera was about to be renewed for another season, my life started to change. One afternoon, about a week before Christmas, I received a call from one of my father's employees. He was "in the neighborhood" and heard that my furnace was broken. He fixed it for free and wished me a merry Christmas. I handed him a calendar, and he pretended to be overjoyed. The next day, the mother of a childhood friend arrived at my door with two of her chickens, plucked and packaged. She said they had extras to give away. Again, I humbly handed her a calendar. More little miracles occurred. A friend brought a box of baby clothes that her boy had outgrown and teased me about my infant son wearing his sister's hand-me-down, pink pajamas. Then, another friend of my mother's arrived with wrapped toys to put under the tree. The doorbell continued to ring, and I received casseroles, offers to babysit, more presents and a bouquet of fresh flowers. I ran out of calendars to give in return.

To this day, I weep every time I think of these simple but loving gestures. Christmas of 1980 was a pivotal time in my life, and I am grateful that I received the true gifts of the season. My precious daughter, so eager to be happy, was amazed at the wonderful sights around our tree. My infant son, a blessing of hope, smiled at me every morning and gave me the determination to switch off the melodrama in my mind. The day before Christmas, my husband was offered a job at an advertising agency in Boise, and we leaped from despair to profound joy. On Christmas Eve, I rocked both babies in my lap and sang them to sleep in heavenly peace. They never noticed my tears falling on their sweet cheeks.

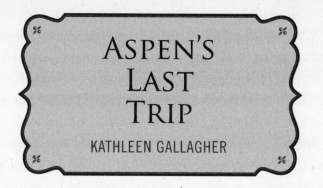

ASPEN'S LAST TRIP

KATHLEEN GALLAGHER

As I rounded the corner into the entrance of Boston's Logan Airport, my heart raced with excitement. Having spotted the Air Canada planes lining the arrival gates, I knew my bundle of joy had landed. "Morning, ma'am," the customs clearance agent greeted me. "We've all been wondering where this puppy was headed. She's been making some strange noises in that crate!" And sure enough, that little puppy was making quite the racket, the same noises that would eventually develop into her talent for talking and holding a squeaky toy in her mouth at the same time. "I think she's going to be a handful," the agent predicted.

I looked into the crate, and there she was—my first glimpse into what the next fourteen years together would bring. My new golden retriever, Aspen, had been flown from Alberta, Canada, to her new home with me. And what a life it would be.

"What a beautiful golden!" a restaurant patron once remarked, catching sight of Aspen outside a café window. Yes, that was my beautiful golden trotting by, having just chewed herself to freedom from the shady tree to which I'd tethered her leash. Aspen led the way in her life, that was certain.

She also loved all food at all times and could never get enough. "The day Aspen stops eating will be the day she is dying," I would sometimes joke to friends as I filled yet another dog bowl. But then there came that day when she didn't finish her meal, and what was once a funny comment became our reality. The vet diagnosed hemangiosarcoma, an aggressive, malignant cancer of the cells that form blood vessels.

Each moment spent with Aspen (yes, even when she was chewing her leash or plunging into a nearby body of water) was always a delight, but became even more so when she underwent surgery for the cancer in November. With Christmas coming, I piled us all into the car, packed to the hilt with not an ounce of space to spare, for our annual holiday road trip home to my parents' house in Maine. Aspen had been an integral part of our family Christmas traditions for the past fourteen years. Each season her stocking hung next to mine, and every year she eagerly tore open her treats and squeaky toys from Santa. Pictures of Aspen with Santa from each season adorned the mantle, and ornaments with the inscription *"Top Dog"* dangled from the tree.

But this Christmas trip was to be very different. It was clear as I set out that Aspen's will to live was ebbing. I hoped that making the trip back East to smell the fresh ocean air would do her good. As much as I tried to deny the odds, I knew in my heart that this would be Aspen's last Christmas. On this holiday trip, I was truly returning home for a special reason. It was time to return one of the greatest gifts in my life to the Giver.

Aspen's demise on the road seemed to happen overnight. Her spirit shifted so quickly from an energetic, inquisitive dog into a shadow of her former self and personality. At a Nebraska truck stop, I crawled into the back seat and held her in my arms, and together we breathed her last breath on that dark, cold winter's night. Carefully and gently, I wrapped her warm body into a soft, blue blanket. On that snowy December evening, I was left with her warm, limp body lying in my arms. Fourteen years of memories instantly melded together. It was a true Christmas miracle that I was fortunate enough to be with her as she lay dying in the back seat.

Aspen was gone. I sat frozen with heartsickness. As I held her, she radiated such a look of happiness and contentment. Her body and face resembled that of a puppy rather than a geriatric dog who had finally succumbed to a debilitating and painful cancer. What was I to do? Sobbing uncontrollably, my mind raced and my thoughts turned to panic. I was nowhere near my final destination of Maine.

What should I do with her dead body? What would someone think if I was found transporting a dead body across state lines? Was there even a vet clinic nearby? Compounding the problem of the situation was that it was only 3:19 a.m. I tried hard to think logically, *I'll wait it out until morning and locate an animal hospital to have her cremated.* I tried to picture that scene, shaking my head. That didn't feel right at all. What did? Home.

I will take her home for Christmas. I climbed back into the front seat and resumed the journey.

The day dawned gray and bleak. There were another cruel eighteen hundred miles ahead. Alone with my devastation, the miles at times felt unbearable. Tears left my eyes blurry, and it was sometimes hard to see the road ahead. My heart felt as frozen as the desolate and snow-covered landscape. A whirlwind of emotion enveloped me as I ventured onward alone. I wanted to turn around, and even more, I longed to go back, back to the beginning of her life.

The rest of the road trip home was somber and tremendously sad, but it offered me the opportunity to say goodbye to Aspen. It was comforting to turn and see her lying on the seat behind me. Each glance in the rearview mirror reflected back the happiness she had given me. As if accompanied by Aspen's spirit, much like a ghost from Christmas past, I embarked on a road trip thousands of miles down memory lane. My mind reverted back to her puppyhood. . . . *Applause filled the room as we received our diploma from puppy kindergarten, which had not proved a huge success for us. Dutifully we had attended each weekly session, but most of the class was spent with Aspen contentedly sleeping in the middle of the training circle while the other puppies pranced around on command. Surprisingly, we managed to graduate due more to her being "cute" than any highly developed skill set; however, the trainer did claim that she had mastered the down position and was the best in the class! Oh, Aspen.*

Here among the crammed-in suitcases and carefully wrapped Christmas presents lay my most treasured and precious gift of all—my beloved golden retriever. Every once in a while, I was startled by stray road noises, certain that what I heard was her in the back seat making her special talking noises and sighs of contentment. It was as though she was talking to me once again, as she had done from that first day at the airport. Each perceived sound garnered a memory from within. *A handful?* I thought, remembering the assessment of the baggage clerk. With an unhesitant smile, I answered, *Yes!*

Each fuel stop afforded me another stolen moment to run my fingers through her silken fur. Her body had now turned cold and rigid. I carefully cradled her paws in my hands. Well-worn rough pads, they had carried her through in life.

At last, there it was, the "Welcome to Maine" road sign. Weary and grateful as I crossed the state line, I became mindfully aware that I had gained more than I had lost on this road trip.

As I reviewed my memories, I knew this was the true meaning of the season. I stopped by the beach with Aspen one last time for her final swim in spirit. A spectacularly blue sky overhead and the sun glistening on the water helped carry the memories of her away.

Aspen truly did go home for Christmas. Only she returned home to stay—this time forever. Our journey home had been spent together, but the journey back was spent alone. The return trip from Maine felt doubly long, and even though the car was packed full, it felt extremely empty. Today, Aspen's spirit lives and travels in my heart wherever I go. And as I head back East for the holidays once again this season, she will be with me throughout the miles. As her ghost of Christmas Future showed me, someday when it comes time for my final journey home, I believe Aspen will be waiting to welcome my spirit home to stay. Until then, I will continue to rejoice in the present.

A SEARS CATALOG CHRISTMAS

LAURA MARTIN

It was a ritual as ritual as the Big Day itself. Before the wind and the storms and the snow and the ice and the freezing cold could encapsulate our tiny lumber town and seal it off from the only known route to civilization (Interstate 5), and on a given Saturday after dinner and seconds and dessert and baths (but before *The Love Boat* and *Fantasy Island*), my father would usher my little brother and me into the tiny, yellow kitchen with the nicotine-stained curtains adorned with dancing tomatoes and dishes from the day piled high and soaking in the sink. It was in this room that we were formally instructed to take a seat at the family dinner table, both of us kids armed with a writing tablet and pen. And in his two hands—behold! Our father bestowed upon us, right smack dab in the middle of the table in all its glossy cover glory, the most magical book in the history of magic books, full of wonder, anticipation, but more important, hope—the Holy Bible of Christmas everywhere—The Sears Wish Book, our family name for the thick Sears catalog. While mom stared at the TV in the living room and the dogs curled up tight on the brick hearth in front of the woodburning stove, my father took one long, lazy drag off the Marlboro dangling from the side of his mouth and—with the echo of his Air Force days behind him—laid out the rules.

"Here's the Sears Christmas Catalog. You kids sit here at the table. You each get ten choices. Write down what you want on the tablet. Here's a pen—you can't erase anything, so make every choice a good one and don't keep crossing stuff out and wasting paper. Write everything down in order of how bad you want it with #1 being what you want the worst. Write down the page number. If you forget the page number, Santa won't know where to find it. Don't write down clothes. Don't write down anything that takes a lot of batteries. Don't write down anything breakable. Don't write down anything heavy. Don't waste your choices on a bunch of expensive stuff. You can each pick out ONE THING that's $20, or you can pick out one BIG THING for $50 that you'll both take turns sharing and not fight over. Doug, don't write down a chemistry set—I don't want you blowing up the house. Don't write down anything that has any liquid in it or anything you need parental supervision to use or anything you're supposed to put bugs in. And Laura, you are NOT sneaking around in the middle of the night making chocolate cakes in your bedroom. Don't write down an Easy-Bake oven. You know, when your grandpa was a kid, his family used to use the pages of the Sears catalog as toilet paper, God's honest truth. Don't get your hopes up that you'll get anything you write down. This isn't a promise you'll get even one thing on your list. You kids have an hour. I'm setting the timer. Let your mom and me know if you're done early, and I don't want to hear any arguing between the two of you coming out of this kitchen."

Ignoring a good portion of these rules, we snuck in high-ticket items under the "To Share" part of our lists, thinking if we feigned a well-behaved, united front, we might just get something really cool. Elaborate walkie-talkie sets—denied. Big Wheel tricycle—denied. Rock tumbler kits—denied. My brother and I even tried the old switcheroo trick by requesting the chemistry set on my list and the Easy-Bake oven on my brother's, but that Santa was too smart a man. Denied.

But—oh!—the joy of opening up that big box containing Barbie's red-and-white VW camper van! Her Dreamhouse may have never come to fruition under our Christmas tree, but Barbie and her pals took many a wonderful adventure with my (extremely tolerant) cat in that van down the hallway, through the living room and across the kitchen linoleum. The blue toy typewriter with the catalog tagline "the perfect gift for little writers" was a dream come true for my wannabe newspaper reporter ten-year-old self, as was the highly coveted cassette tape recorder I carted around everywhere to record anything that anyone wanted to say.

As an adult, I grew to distance myself from the consumer side of Christmas as the importance of "things" became trite and even a bit silly. My yearly holiday list is now a suitcase-packing check-off list as my partner and I head out of town far, far away from family, friends and the conspicuous consumption of Christmas. Our destination—the central coast, where he and I trade stuff for memories and swap expectation for relaxation. (It's amazing how much we've grown to enjoy—and I mean REALLY enjoy—holiday music without the worry of a checking account shrinking out of control.)

I admit, however, that I really do like making lists, and admittedly, I've been known to use some of this holiday downtime to indulge in lists for the upcoming new year: home improvement lists, untried recipes and unread book lists, lists of lists that still need to be made, the writing down, the crossing out, the foregoing of pen for pencil and discovering the joys that a pink, nubby eraser can truly bring. Of course, I never call these resolutions, and I don't get my hopes up high enough to actually finish anything on these lists. I don't even take them too seriously either, remembering that as long as I always put what I want the worst at the very top, somehow everything else simply—and inevitably—falls right into place.

CHRISTMAS WITHOUT SNOW

ROSI HOLLINBECK

Living in Minnesota has some drawbacks: the sweltering dog days of August filled with mosquitoes the size of Buicks, and Februarys that seem to freeze even time. But one of the true joys of being a Minnesotan is being there at Christmastime. It just seems so right. Minnesota is a Christmas kind of place. Cheeks and nose tips redden in crisp, cold air. Soft, fresh snow nearly always blankets the ground on Christmas mornings. Frost covers everything, turning trees and bushes into jeweled ice sculptures. The daytime sky is such a pure, hard blue that it hurts to look at it, and the sun casts purple shadows across the snow. The sweet smell of burning hardwood permeates the air through the long evenings.

It was 1961, and I was fifteen years old. I had never been away from home during that joyous time around Christmas. And this wasn't just any Christmas. This was to be the first Christmas for my first niece. Well, it was not technically her first Christmas. She had been born on Christmas Day one year earlier. Robin was a most special child, as special as her day of birth. She was as bright and beautiful and full of joy as Christmas. I had looked forward to this, her first real Christmas, since the day she was born.

A friend who had a very complete woodworking shop had used his jigsaw to cut out the pieces so I could make a little maple rocking horse for her. I sanded every surface until it was smooth as a river rock and every edge was sanded round. There would be no rough spots or sharp edges on Robin's rocking horse. I painted it a deep, rich red and added features in midnight black. This would be a special gift for such a wonderful little girl. I had worked on it for weeks and couldn't wait to see her face on Christmas morning.

But that first Christmas for Robin would be stolen from me. My parents decided to take a winter vacation to Florida, and I had to go with them. I could stay with my sister, I argued. You will go with us, they insisted. The choir is doing a concert at the shopping center, I pleaded. They can do it without you, they answered. But this is where I want to be, I begged. You belong with us at Christmas, they said. Their minds were made up. Florida! No winter. No snow crunching under my boots. No mailman bringing packages to rattle from relatives in Chicago or a case of oranges from my uncle in California. No snow angels or toboggans flying down hills or snowball wars. But most important of all, no Robin on Christmas morning.

My parents had bought an old bread truck and outfitted it with beds and a camp kitchen. It was bulky, ugly and not at all comfortable. The heat didn't work well, and the only window was the windshield. Visiting distant cousins and dreary friends along the way, we showered in their homes and slept in our makeshift camper parked in their driveways and yards. Each day took us farther from where I wanted to be. Robin would be toddling around in new rubber boots, amazed at the sparkling lights under the eaves, red-nosed in the snow, sledding down the backyard hill in someone else's lap. We would spend Christmas in the Florida Everglades in a campground bordered by palm trees and surrounded, no doubt, by snakes and alligators and overly tan people in plaid Bermuda shorts and sandals. In my fifteen-year-old's mind, it couldn't be any worse.

I was mad. Madder than mad. And I acted like your typical angry teenager. I sat in the truck, read books and wrote dejected letters home. I couldn't write letters to Robin, though. She wouldn't know what they were. She would just know I wasn't there. I never looked out the windshield at any of the sights. I was determined not to enjoy one single minute of this miserable trip. I sulked at a medal-winning Olympic level.

Somehow we'd gotten behind schedule and found ourselves in a little town in southern Georgia on Christmas Eve. There were a few people about, but it seemed so foreign to me. Not only was it warm and there was no snow, but everyone there was African American. Minnesota didn't have a very diverse population in those days, and I had never met a black person before. I was in a place where nothing, not even the people, was in any way familiar.

It was late and we needed to find gas. Only one place in this tiny town was still open—a small store attached to a gas station on the south edge of town. A young African American man, not that much older than I was, pumped gas into the huge tank of the bread truck, nodding as my father chatted. Mom began making supper: bologna sandwiches on white bread with mustard. At home, we would have had a long table buried under mounds of Swedish meatballs, sliced ham, hot German potato salad, plates of pickled herring, sweet brown bread, rice pudding and more. This year, we would have bologna sandwiches for Christmas dinner.

I thought my teeth would break from gritting them. I had to get out of the truck, so I jumped down and strode into the store. It was a small place with few items on the broad, wooden shelves, but everything was tidy and clean. Three tiny, chocolate-skinned children stared at me from behind the counter, eyes wide with wonder at a white person in their store. The smallest put his fingers in his mouth and hid behind his mother's skirt, peeking up at me. His mother, a young woman not much older than

I was, spoke with a heavy drawl. Her voice was as soft and sweet as caramel. "Merry Christmas, honey. Can I help you find anything?" Her broad, friendly smile beamed at me, and her kind eyes crinkled at the corners.

I was too angry to be nice. "No. I don't want anything. I just want to be away from *them!*" I wagged my head toward my parents. It was as if something broke open inside me, and I kept on talking. "I don't want to be here. I want to be home for Christmas! I want to be with the rest of my family and my friends. I should be in Minnesota. That's where I belong." Tears sprang to my eyes, and I turned, fleeing back to the truck. Fighting against the tears, I sat on my bed with arms crossed hard over my chest, my trembling chin jutted out.

It seemed to take forever for that gas tank to fill, but finally Dad paid the young man for the gas, and I heard them wish each other a merry Christmas. Dad climbed onto the driver's seat and started the engine. A sharp rapping came at his window. He rolled the door open, and a hand pushed a Christmas box into his hands. They passed a few quiet words, and Dad looked back at me. Then he said to the person outside the truck, "Thank you, and you have a Merry Christmas, too," before closing the door and driving away.

Mom took a sandwich and Coke to Dad and, when she came back, handed me the box. "This is for you. The woman in the store brought it out."

I stared at it for a long time, touching the worn corners of a well-used Christmas box, picking at an old, yellowed piece of tape on one edge. Finally, I wiggled the red yarn tied around it and opened the box, taking care not to tear it, knowing instinctively that it should be saved. The sharp aroma of evergreen filled the truck. Inside lay a pine branch hung with a couple of handmade paper ornaments and draped with a short string of popcorn, the end of the branch crudely cut. A Baby Ruth candy bar lay in the box next to a folded piece of notebook paper.

"Those who you love are always in your heart, with you wherever you go. Think of them now and have a Merry Christmas." Then I cried, really cried, with a gush of tears and deep, gulping sobs. Not for me, but for the chance I'd wasted to share a few words, a Christmas wish and a little time with a truly kind and generous woman, a woman who had no snow crunching under her feet or jeweled ice on her trees but knew the true meaning of Christmas far better than I.

CIRCLE
OF LOVE

VALERIE
REYNOSO PIOTROWSKI

As we grow older, we come to realize that one of the genuine gifts of childhood is the magical way that a small child views even the simplest thing. The memory of opening our first pop-up book, finding the hidden toy in the Cracker Jack box or even riding a bike without training wheels—each of these events seems like magic at the time.

Much of the magic in my early years was provided by the gifts of my two glamorous aunts, Aunt Lupe and Aunt Mary. My mother, Vivian, was one of twelve children of a pear-farming family in the Sacramento River Delta. Her sisters lavished toys and attention on my sister and me; we were the appreciative beneficiaries of their undivided love and devotion.

Aunt Lupe was particularly exotic. She lived in Palm Springs, and to a seven-year-old like me, that seemed the very pinnacle of sophistication and elegance. Her frequent letters and postcards were exciting and colorful and told of fancy parties, perpetually sunny skies and swimsuit weather, and frequent sightings of famous movie stars. Like clockwork, the gifts from Palm Springs would arrive for our birthdays and at Christmas. Her carefully selected gifts brought joy and contentment to our young lives. Someone from far away loved and cherished us, and it made us feel tremendously special.

In the mid-1960s, Aunt Lupe truly outdid herself. Showing the sixth sense she seemed to have for our interests, that year she sent us each a beautiful satin-ivory jewelry box with hand-painted pink flowers and gold trim. When the box was opened, a delicate plastic ballerina spun around on one foot to the tune of "The Blue Danube" waltz.

But there was an even more wonderful surprise tucked inside the pink satin lining: a piece of costume jewelry, a Christmas pin that was the most perfect thing I had ever seen in my short life. It was in the shape of an old-fashioned Christmas tree, like a Currier & Ives Christmas card tree, framed by a snow-tinged window on a winter's night. Its enamel branches were laced with "snow," and semiprecious stones were scattered in abundance from top to bottom. The tip of the tree was crowned with a gold star with a crystal in the middle. To this day, I cannot think about that pin without feeling the love and security I felt as a young child and realizing how fortunate I was to have someone who thought that I was special enough to merit this sparkling treasure. It was pure magic.

Through the years and the Christmas seasons to come, my prized Christmas tree pin was an annual adornment. I pinned it to college blazers, to the red wool cape that I had sewn myself and to the first grown-up houndstooth jacket I purchased to celebrate my appointment to a political position. I so treasured the pin and the memories it contained of Christmases past that I neither checked my coat nor let it out of my sight during its holiday forays.

In 1988, I attended my boss's Christmas party in the company of the man I had been dating since our sophmore year in high school, Kevin. Naturally, I wore my Christmas pin. The combination of pink champagne and the frustration at our unresolved relationship brought the evening to an early and tearful close. I went home that night alone and unhappy.

As I sobbed alone in my house, I decided that if I immediately hung up my party dress and put away my holiday coat and purse, then perhaps I would have no physical memory of this night the following morning. It was as I was hanging up my black velvet duster that I noticed—the Christmas pin that had been with me for almost twenty years, for almost two-thirds of my life, was gone.

I searched my car. It wasn't there. Frantic, I called my boss and asked him to look around his house. No, came the reply ten minutes later, it was not to be found at his house. Despite my broken heart and the thirty-degree weather on that foggy night, I pulled a coat over my flannel nightgown and drove fifteen miles to my boss's house in my bunny slippers, armed with a flashlight and my prayers that the pin would be laying there on the sidewalk. I searched the surrounding neighborhood for forty-five minutes, but the pin was gone. And gone, too, were my cozy feelings of Christmas love.

The loss of the pin ushered in one of the darkest periods of my life. The breast cancer that had ravaged my beautiful mother for almost ten years was now winning its evil campaign to take her life, and through rivers of tears and counseling, I also realized that Kevin and I did not have the kind of future together that I both wanted and deserved. The prospect of those two losses occurring simultaneously in my life was unbearable. I found solace in myriad work projects, but I was scared to death. My father's grief at the approaching loss of his life partner, coupled with Kevin's emotional absence, left me alone to deal with my fears.

Christmas of 1989 would be the last one we would spend with my mom. Through a miracle of God, she was released from the hospital in time to attend Aunt Mary's traditional tamale dinner. I witnessed the joy in her eyes each moment she spent in the company of the family; I am truly grateful for my mom having had the strength to endure what would be her last Christmas season with us. She was storing up her own memories to reflect on during her quiet times in heaven.

My mother left this life just a few short months after that. Despite months of counseling before her death, nothing could have prepared me for the hopelessness I felt following her passing. There were entire days spent in my pajamas. I had lost half of my life base, and I did not know how to continue being the self-assured, ambitious young woman she had raised me to be.

But the darkness of winter passed, and spring finally arrived, and with it the annual invitation to visit the beach house of Aunt Mary and Uncle Roger. My childhood was filled with summer memories of white sand, starfish and walks with my parents on the beaches of Pajaro Dunes. The beach house was the last place I thought I could endure at this moment in my life. But Aunt Mary began to wear down my objections. She was grieving, too, she pointed out, and returning to the very spot where we had enjoyed so many good times would be therapeutic to us all.

And so I agreed to go. Surprisingly, the drive itself offered peace of mind, and as the odometer registered the passing miles, my sense of tranquility increased. Maybe Aunt Mary knew something that I didn't, something about facing our fears and healing.

At the beach house that year, Aunt Mary and I found common ground in the love and loss of my mom, her sister and best friend. We spent hours sitting on the beach, laughing and crying through our stories and recollections of summers past. On the last day of the trip, I awoke with a feeling of rejuvenation. It had been so long since I'd had any energy that I assumed this burst I was feeling was due to the ocean air. I had no idea then that I had passed one of the most important tests of grieving, six months after losing Mom. I had returned to the scene of happy family times and faced painful memories.

The drive back to Sacramento began peacefully. I was in no hurry to get back, as I felt so serene and didn't want to jeopardize this newfound calm. Impulsively, I stopped at a little town near Pajaro, where Main Street consisted of a block of antique shops. It was early morning, and some shops had not yet opened their doors.

The last antique shop on the right side of the street was open for business, though, and as I stepped in, I recognized the musty odor of old furniture and well-used books. Through the maze of Victorian lamps and curio cabinets filled with silver spoons and other standard antique fare, I spotted the jewelry case at the back of the store. Perhaps there was some small trinket there that I could take away to remind me of my newfound strength.

I have always believed that things happen for a reason, and what I saw then affirmed my belief. There, tucked in a corner on an old piece of velvet, was the twin to the Christmas tree pin I had lost one year before. I asked the shopkeeper to remove it from the display case and, with trembling hands, turned the little pin over. Yes, this was it, the very same company name inscribed on the back of the pin. In a miracle of rediscovery, I had found the one tangible thing I valued most, a treasure from my beloved past.

Although there was much work to be done emotionally for me and my family, I was now firmly on the way to healing. The boundlessness of the seashore, with waves breaking one after another for all eternity, and the Christmas pin that held within its branches so many feelings of warmth and love were again returned to me. In the years to come, I would face other losses and disappointments, but now I knew that I possessed the strength and support from my circle of family and friends that would protect me and sustain my recovery whenever I needed them. And my holiday symbol of love, my Christmas pin, would again accompany me into another year of life.

MALL SANTA

DAVID SCOTT CHAMBERLAIN,
AS TOLD TO BARBARA CHAMBERLAIN

My senior year in high school, my goal in life was to get closer to my perfect woman. Teddy Martin always seemed to be in a gaggle of girls. She would return my smiles, but one or another of her friends always seemed to be in the way of a real conversation. I am not ashamed to admit that one November day I eavesdropped and heard her talking to her friends about her Christmas job as an elf at the mall. Immediately, I decided to try there for some kind of holiday work. The last year of high school was expensive, I could use some extra money . . . and if I could be near blue-eyed, blonde-haired Theodora Martin, it would be a dream come true.

The human resources woman at the mall stared at me from behind her desk. "How tall are you?"

Okay, at 6'2" I was probably not elf material. "I could do stock work," I offered, hopeful. My dream seemed to be slipping away.

"We've already hired for most jobs, but there is someone we still need," she offered. "We need someone to give our Santa breaks. It is only a total of three hours a day, but if you want that job . . ."

Three hours a day near Elf Teddy? And I would be paid? Frosting on my cake. A paycheck for handing out candy canes and saying, "Ho ho ho." I smiled and nodded in agreement. Santa was the job for me.

"Let's see how you look in the Santa suit," Mrs. HR said. Even more of a bonus, Teddy helped me with the suit. "Oh, Davey, you look great!" She helped adjust the beard. "Our Santa has a real white beard, but you look good. And you're taller than he is. How tall are you?"

My day, week and year were complete.

My assignment the first day was to observe. The line of kiddies seemed to be like that eternally full bowl of rice in a fable. They were there before Santa's appointed hour and groaned when Elf Teddy or one of the other elves put up the "Santa's Gone to the North Pole" sign at 8:30 p.m.

It is a well-known fact that candy canes turn into syrup in the hands of anyone under age eight. Why some mothers insisted on terrifying their children by dumping them on my lap in spite of wails from the offspring was a mystery. During my noontime assignments, I often thought that I might lose my hearing. It was worth it to hear Teddy say, "You are so good with the children."

One day, the full-time Santa didn't come back from lunch.

He was half an hour late when I told Teddy to put up the closed sign.

I could hear the snore from outside the door of the employee lounge. The form in the red suit was on the couch, his genuine round belly rising and falling with each snore. I shook his shoulder gently. He snorted, sat up and cried, "Bring on the kiddies!" and fell back onto the couch to begin the wall-rocking snore again. Santa had obviously had more than milk and cookies for lunch.

Just then, the woman who had hired me opened the door. "Where is Santa? The kids and moms are getting restless out there."

Santa bolted up and began an off-key rendition of "Jingle Bells."

"Oh, no," she groaned, understanding the situation immediately. "David, you are going to have to finish as Santa today."

And that was how I became the mall's youngest ever first-string Santa Claus. Anyone who thinks that being a Santa is an easy job should just try it. It's easier to be a football lineman, take it from me. But out of it, I got a paycheck, and yes, I got Teddy. She agreed to be my date for the senior prom, which was about the greatest Christmas present Santa ever brought me.

THE
BABY
FLIGHT

PAUL KARRER

I had never held such an unusual looking baby in my arms before. To tell the truth, I had never even seen an infant like this before. Now, here I was, responsible for delivering three tiny orphans to their adoptive parents on Christmas Eve.

Twenty-eight years old, a New England Yankee through and through, I taught English on Cheju Island, Republic of Korea. College students all over the country had been rioting and had succeeded in closing colleges. I was fed up and needed to go home, but I was short of money. One of my colleagues informed me of the "baby flights," whereby I could travel from Korea to the United States and back for a mere twenty-five percent of the normal fare. But there was a hitch. The traveler had to transport not one, not two, but three infants. That translated into at least three flight changes—Tokyo, Anchorage and New York, in my case. I would have to bring diapers, formula, pacifiers and much patience. The alternative was to pay the full fare.

I found myself boarding a plane with three infants, ages three months, seven months and a year and a half. They came complete with runny noses and wet diapers.

When the plane finally took off, the poor kids let loose with a terrible howl. As the plane climbed, it began to vibrate violently. In unison, all three babies quieted. A few seconds later, the plane stopped shaking, and in unison, the babies resumed crying. The entire planeload of passengers burst into tension-relieving laughter. And that made my tiny charges instant celebrities.

But one thing had given me pause the entire time. The eighteen-month-old infant, quieter than the other two, had a massive head with disproportionately minute arms and fingers. Obviously, the poor thing was affected with dwarfism. My reaction surprised me. I was repulsed and began to worry whether the new parents on the other side of the Pacific realized what they were having delivered to them. I didn't look forward to the transfer, but I was too busy to give it much consideration.

Babies were hollering. The one on my lap was wet, and the milk formula was low. I rapidly learned how to clean a wet bottom, put on a new diaper and stick a pacifier in an open mouth.

Two American marines stopped in the aisle near me and stared down.

"You look like you could use a little help."

"I could. Three kids is a lot."

"Mind if we each take one for a few minutes?"

"No, I wouldn't mind at all." I happily passed a baby to each of them and watched the massive soldiers coo to the babies.

So, I sat there alone, holding the eighteen-month-old baby with the very large head. I noticed her long eyelashes. As I looked into her eyes, I couldn't help but see that they held a crisp, intelligent glow. Then, she smiled, and I was hooked. Funny how things like that can change you. From that point on, she radiated beauty, and she never left my arms.

In Tokyo, the plane had a stopover. The soldiers apologized for not being able to help anymore, as they had another flight. They each handed back a baby. I placed two babies in a twin stroller and carried the third in my arms. The four of us plunked down in a waiting area. I started to change the diapers of the two babies I had given to the soldiers, when a pile of single dollar bills fell from one of the baby's clothing. I quickly glanced at the departing soldiers. One of them gave the thumbs-up sign and blurted, "Little buggers gonna need all the help they can get. Merry Christmas."

Not many minutes later, an attractive Asian woman approached, stared at us and walked away. I rocked a baby as two fidgeted. The woman walked up again and stared.

"Are those babies yours?"

"No, I'm delivering them. They're Korean orphans."

"I thought so. Twenty-four years ago, I was one of those kids. I think we are on the same flight. May I please help you?"

She took the noisiest child of the three. During the flight, she'd show up and lend a hand, clean a bottom or soothe an unsettled little one. Finally, she took one infant, walked down the aisle, and I didn't see her until the plane landed.

By now, I had developed a strong bond with "my" baby. I even named her Tina. The more I thought about giving her to someone else, the more I worried about her prospective parents. I felt like a slave trader and a traitor all wrapped into one.

In New York, the plane landed. People rushed in, matched identification tags, and off they sped with their new children. But I still held Tina, and it seemed like nobody was coming on board for her. In the end, I trudged off the plane to a small crowd. Tina clung to me tightly and cried.

Then I spotted them, standing to the side of the exit. The man was no more than four feet tall, and his wife was even tinier. They walked toward me and reached up for Tina. As I passed Tina to them, she looked up at me and said, "Oma," to me, which means mom in Korean. At that point, I cried.

The next year, I paid the full fare. The baby flight was too expensive.

CHILDHOOD MAGIC

JO ANNE BOULGER

I grew up in southern California many years ago. After I married, my husband and I lived in several different states and had a child in each of our first four states. As I continued this pattern—four states, four babies—I worried about the fact that there were fifty states. Was I going for a world record? Fortunately, in the fifth state in which we lived, we broke the pattern. We left there after seven years without adding to our family.

During these times away from home, my father was involved with the construction of Disneyland. Because we lived in Washington state, we missed out on all the action, including the day before Disneyland was officially opened to the public, when my father, his family and all the other workers and their families were welcomed as guests of Disneyland. They were given a memorial plate, along with Mickey Mouse watches for the children and a day of free rides and all the meals they could eat.

So when we came home for a vacation, my father was anxious to share the excitement of Disneyland with his grandchildren. He was so proud of his part in the construction and eager to be our host and share his love of the park. We drove to Anaheim in anticipation of a world of excitement and magic.

My parents hadn't seen their grandchildren for some time, and I was eager for my children to be on their best behavior. Fingers crossed, we entered the park. The magic castle took our breath away, and we all stopped and took in our surroundings. The children were sidetracked by the characters from the many different nursery rhymes; right before our eyes, storybooks came alive. There was Sleeping Beauty, Mickey Mouse, Minnie Mouse and many others, all life-size.

Then it happened—along came the Big Bad Wolf chasing the Three Little Pigs, squealing like crazy. My five-year-old son, Quin, reacted immediately. He ran straight up to the Big Bad Wolf and punched him in the stomach. Sadly for the young man wearing the costume, a five-year-old's swinging fist lands quite a bit short, more in the groin area. It was a hard punch below the belt for the Big Bad Wolf.

The wolf keeled over and fell to his knees. Everyone around us looked on in shock, and my parents were aghast at their grandchild's outrageous behavior. My son shocked me, too—he was a very sweet boy, not in the least bit mean.

With a face red with embarrassment, I grabbed his arm. "What are you doing? Why did you hit the wolf?"

Quin looked up at me proudly. "To save the Three Little Pigs."

Oh, not a bully, but a hero in the making. My husband went to the aid of the fallen wolf while I reprimanded our son. This was really hard for me to do because I knew how kindhearted my son really was, yet I couldn't let it just pass as though nothing had happened. But I was proud of my son wanting to be a hero. It was at this time that I explained to him about the costume and the young man he had decked. The conversation did not sit well with him. On the way home, he started to ask more questions: If the Big Bad Wolf was just a kid in a costume, then what about all the other magic moments in his life? What about the Easter Bunny, the Tooth Fairy, even Santa Claus? I answered as best I could, dancing around the issue.

As we drove home, I sadly looked out the window at the passing scene. *What had I done to my son by taking away all the childhood magic?* Come Christmas, I knew I needed to do something to convince him of the magic in believing.

On Christmas Eve, I had all three children leave milk and cookies for Santa. That night, I made a note written with glue and sprinkled with red glitter signed with a big S for Santa. This worked wonders, and he was once again a believer. After all, only Santa could write with glittering red ink.

The following year, I worked extra hard for Easter, the Tooth Fairy and some Halloween goblins. I did my utmost to convince Quin of all the magic of the moment.

That next Christmas, we visited Santa Claus. Quin, now six years old, was eager to sit on Santa's lap. During his conversation with Santa, Quin's enthusiasm took him away again, and he put his hand on Santa's fake beard and gave it a big yank, gathering a handful of Santa's fluffy, white beard.

Oh, no, I thought, shocked by what he had done. *I guess he's on to the whole Santa thing. He really no longer believes.* It looked as though he were trying to prove something by yanking the beard, letting the rest of us know he would no longer fall for our make-believe stories. It made me sad to think that my young son had really lost the magic of childhood. At the same time, I was mortified by his actions. I stood frozen and red-faced, certain that all the other mothers were also shocked and worried that he was setting a very bad example for their children.

Luckily for Santa and me, the beard was well attached, and there was no harm done. I guess he had been through this before and used really good glue, so he just sat there with his face as red as his suit.

Quin ran up to me happily, a big smile on his face, holding a handful of Santa's beard.

"Look, Mom, I've got some of Santa's beard to hang on our Christmas tree for good luck."

I looked at Santa, and he gave me a wink, tapped the side of his nose with his finger and, with a big smile, waved us goodbye.

SILENT NIGHT

LIZA LONG

We waited, our noses pressed into strangers' backs as if we were lost children in a crowded subway car. The air smelled of wet woolen coats, and the snow fell in silence, tickling our eyelashes and melting when it brushed our reddened, mittenless hands.

We were strangers to snow, a family of six children and two parents from southern California, waiting with thousands of other grumpy, chilled people at Temple Square in Salt Lake City, Utah, one Thanksgiving evening for the Christmas lights to come on. Already the winter shadows were deepening. We waited expectantly for something to happen.

No lights. "Don't worry, children," my father said, rubbing his hands together and blowing on them. "They'll come on as soon as it's dark. It will be worth the wait. You'll see." His breath blew out in a cloud, like a cartoon character. We nodded silently, squirming as unfamiliar elbows and knees jostled and poked us. Everyone around us was complaining now, a low, grumbling, wordless sound. Still there were no lights. And it was dark now.

The unpleasant rumbling grew louder. We caught snatches here and there, words that expressed sentiments very close to what we ourselves were feeling.

"I want to go home," one child, captured in his mother's arms, whined pitiably.

"You'd think they'd be more organized," grumbled a deep voice at my shoulder.

"Come on!" one young man yelled. "Turn on the stupid lights already!"

I looked at my white-faced brothers and sister, realizing that they felt as cold and miserable as I did. "Some Christmas lights," I said sarcastically under my breath.

And then, I heard the song. I looked up, surprised at first, then embarrassed, as my father began to sing. His rich, full baritone rang through the sudden hush that surrounded us, warming the cold winter with its golden sound. "Silent night," he sang, "holy night. All is calm, all is bright." As he sang that lovely tune, those simple words, the lights came on as if on command, a brilliant display of colors and beauty to welcome the Christmas season. A few more voices filled the air, then still more joined in harmony—first two parts, then three, then four, and soon I realized that everyone around us had joined my father's song.

I felt like one of the shepherds two thousand years ago, transfixed by heavenly choirs heralding a new birth and a new world. As we made our way around the beautiful grounds, Dad kept singing, and many of the strangers around us joined in as he moved effortlessly from one favorite Christmas carol to the next. People who had been cold and miserable moments before were warmed and transformed by the music. Suddenly, we were all friends, neighbors, fellow worshipers.

A few months later, Dad became ill. Three years later, after a long struggle with cancer, he passed away. His most powerful lessons live on, though. I have never forgotten the beauty of that "Silent Night" so many years ago, and the appreciation for the true spirit of Christmas that he shared with his family and strangers will always remain in my heart.

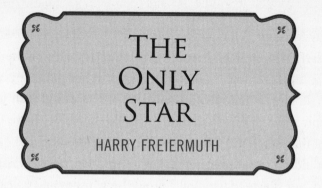

THE ONLY STAR

HARRY FREIERMUTH

During World War II, Christmas was crucial for keeping our spirits up. Our street's air raid warden would ring our doorbell if any light showed through our windows at night. For that reason, we used light-proof window shades or thick blankets to cover our windows to keep the slightest ray of light from escaping and telling the enemy planes where we were. We never knew if this Christmas might be our last. Already enemy submarines had been sighted near our coast. How soon would enemy planes reach our coastal cities and towns, just as they had bombed Pearl Harbor on December 7, 1941?

Wartime or not, we young people had to go to school. During my freshman year, 1942, at Watsonville Joint Union High School in Watsonville, California, I worked after school and Saturdays at Ford's Department Store on Main Street.

I was Assistant Window Dresser First Class. The head window dresser, Miss Grahame, would brush her red hair from her grey-green eyes and say, "Harry, please go and bring the new adult female blonde mannequin to window 3." I would rush to the supply room to find the blonde with the big, blue, Bette Davis eyes that dared any woman to buy what she modeled. Then, I would put my strong right arm around her naked waist and carry her slowly to window 3 amid the whistles and catcalls of the male clerks. As a teenager, I tried my best to keep everything on a purely professional level, while inside my ego glowed and smiled triumphantly.

Christmas was our busiest time of the year. Besides outstanding clothes and eye-catching signs, our window was filled with beautiful Christmas trees with the newest sparkling glass ornaments in all colors and twinkling electric lights in all shapes and sizes—the great temptation to entice our customers to buy buy buy.

I looked at our finished windows and, in my mind's eye, compared these trees to my family's traditional little tree with its old-fashioned ornaments and electric light bulbs that were always burning out, causing us to spend what seemed like hours trying to find the burnt-out bulb.

On December 7, 1942, my mother's birthday, Dad took Mother, my younger brother, Gene, and me in his pickup truck to buy our family tree. In the tree lot on East Lake Avenue, we found a five-foot tree that would look like it was seven feet on top of our small coffee table.

Once home, Gene and I carried our tree inside and placed it on top of the coffee table in front of our front window covered with a thick blanket. The fragrant fir branches gave off their perfume, giving us all a taste of Christmas No. 5. I breathed deep to enjoy this tree's special gift to us. Mother brought the old cardboard box from her bedroom closet shelf and placed it on the carpet in front of our tree. We always offered to help her with this annual ritual. But she did not want anyone to see all of her treasures hidden in her special closet. Only later would I discover just what each one meant to her.

Gene and I began unwrapping the old tissue paper covering each ornament. When we discovered which ornament we had unwrapped, we squinted at our tree to see where it should find its traditional place. Then, we hung it on that branch, just where it should always be this year and every year.

Mother and Dad sat together on our chesterfield sofa, watching Gene and me decorate our tree. If we did not get an ornament in its exact right place, we heard about it fast. And just as fast, we made the correction. Our Christmas star was the first ornament to grace our new tree. This five-pointed star, four inches across from point to point, was a flat piece of aluminum. We wired it to the top of the tree where it lighted the way for the Three Wise Men to find the Christ Child.

The Christ Child was in a small paper manger, a heavy paper foldout held together by tape, and he was placed carefully at the bottom trunk of our tree. Jesus, Mary and Joseph rested peacefully on the manger straw surrounded by the shepherds and their sheep. The ox and the donkey poked their heads through a back window. On the two sides of the stable were the Three Wise Men. Two stood on the right side, and one knelt on the left side in adoration.

Gene placed the crayon-colored, paper Santa Claus halfway up the trunk of our tree. From that lofty position, Santa smiled to everyone and held his big bag of gifts for all. I attached the blue bird, a peacock with a worn-out feathery tail, by the clip under its feet to the branch about one-third of the way up the tree. It looked about ready to take off for a safer place to land. One by one, we unwrapped each ornament and returned it to its rightful place on this year's Christmas tree. Every year, the routine had been the same throughout my childhood.

Next to last, we unwrapped the strings of popcorn from their cardboard and strung each one very gracefully, beginning from the very top of the tree down to the bottom branches. Gene and I remembered popping this very popcorn many years ago in our old wire-mesh popcorn popper in the front room fireplace. We had to shake the popper to move the kernels around so they did not burn in the flames of the fire.

As soon as we had finished with the popcorn, Gene began stringing the electric lights down from the top of the tree around and around to the bottom. Then, we hung the tinsel icicles on the ends of each branch of our tree. Finally, we turned out all the lights and sat in the darkened room. With fingers crossed, I turned on the switch for our Christmas tree lights.

"Hooray!" The lights all lit up okay. No burnt-out bulbs so far.

This was a silent moment for our family. In the quiet tree light, our tree wished each of us a very merry Christmas. And without saying a word, we thanked our tree and wished it, and one another, a merry Christmas too.

* * *

That night in bed, before falling asleep, an unusual sparkling thought blossomed in the back of my freshman brain: *Why not change that old-fashioned Christmas tree with its worn-out ornaments for a tree full of the newest glistening ornaments from Ford's Department Store?*

* * *

The next day at work, I purchased the most expensive glass ornaments in my favorite colors, chartreuse and magenta, a fantastic improvement on the old traditional red and green for Christmas colors. I complemented that brainstorm with another brainstorm and bought yellow and purple twinkling electric lights in the shapes of bells and stars. I could not wait to change our old ornaments for these fabulous new ones. And catch the expressions of surprise and wonder on the faces of Mother, Dad and Gene.

I carried the big surprise home secretly in a big, plain paper bag and hid it in my bedroom closet. I waited for a time when everyone was out of the house. Then, secretly and unknowingly, I committed the Christmas crime of the century.

After supper, it was our custom to go, in the dark, into our living room. Mother and Dad would sit on the chesterfield sofa while Gene and I would lie flat on the floor and listen to our favorite radio program, *I Love a Mystery*. We delighted in the thrills and masterminds of Jack, Doc and Reggie, along with the spine-chilling screams of Mercedes McCambridge.

After all of that excitement and before anyone could turn on the lights, I lit my masterpiece. Total silence. No one said a word. The silence roared in my ears. Finally, Mother looked at my smiling face with her tender, light blue eyes and asked, "Harry, did you do this?"

"Yes," I admitted.

"WHY?" they all shouted together.

Mother, still with a soft and tender voice, said, "Harry, we know you must have had a good intention. But, our old, dilapidated Christmas tree ornaments hold memories that money cannot buy. I thought you already knew that.

"The aluminum star was designed and cut out by hand by your dear father for our first Christmas tree, after our marriage in 1925. It pointed the way for imaginary Wise Men to find the imaginary Christ Child at the foot of our first Christmas tree. The paper Santa Claus was hand drawn by your little brother, when he was in kindergarten. He was so proud of his work that we had to find a special place for it. We did, right on our family Christmas tree."

She looked at my father sitting next to her. "Each year, your father and I would buy a new ornament to remember something special in our lives. We bought the blue bird with the feathery tail the year you were born, 1927. And remember when you were sick in fourth grade? We could not have any parties in the house for a year because Dr. Giberson thought that you had TB and must have complete rest for a full year. That was the year we bought the musical ornament that plays 'Silent Night.'"

I hung my head. My moment of triumph had become a moment of shame. She smiled lovingly, "Yes, I could go on. But you can see how much our family Christmas tree means to us. I thought you knew that, too."

"Oh, yes," I cried with tears in my eyes. "Please, forgive me. Now I understand why these ornaments are family treasures."

"We forgive you and love you. Now take those ornaments off and put our old family ornaments back where they belong."

***

Dad died in 1968 after six years of battling Lou Gehrig's disease, and Mother tried to decorate our family Christmas tree alone that year. Gene and I were grown up and on our own. As soon as her wrinkled and trembling hands touched the aluminum star, she wept. After rewrapping the star in its wrinkled tissue paper, Mother placed it carefully in its place in the old cardboard box, closed the lid, placed the box back on the shelf of her bedroom closet and closed the door. That year, our family Christmas tree disappeared forever. But, in my heart, Dad's homemade star will always point toward the infant Jesus.

VIRTUAL CHRISTMAS

PAT HANSON

I prefer Halloween to Christmas. You have an excuse for putting on a mask, can dress up any way you'd like and just pretend. Soon after, when retailers start luring us with Christmas decorations, recorded mall music everywhere plays carols, television repeats all those sappy movies . . . All that jolliness can make me feel a little depressed. Some Christmases are more difficult than others, but one that could have been a catastrophe instead forever transformed how our family celebrates December 25.

It was 1996, the day before the office Christmas party, when my boss called me in to his office and gave me thirty days' notice. Since summer, I'd been the sole support of my teenage stepson and my husband, after his plumbing business tanked. Credit cards at their limit, stretched by one income, we'd done no Christmas shopping and hadn't even bought a tree. I didn't know how I would be able to get into the holiday cheer and forget the reality of my financial situation. Tears ran down my cheeks on the way home as the car radio reminded listeners that there were only six shopping days left, and the shrill voices of the Chipmunks sang, *"Christmas, Christmas time is here, time to sing, time for cheer."*

Somehow that week, out of the depths of my despair, I got an idea. We'd have a virtual Christmas. We'd each find and wrap pictures of five gifts we would have been thoughtful and generous enough to buy had there been money to put into circulation! And central to this plan was that one of the virtual gifts had to be intangible, like a quality within that you'd like the other to have.

Three days before Christmas, I hid the stockings. Instead of a big, traditional tree, we decorated our ficus tree with lights. We each looked through catalogs, magazines and our hearts to choose five presents for one another and place them under the tree. In addition to the gifts of a car, a driver's license, a baggy sweatshirt and pants and guitar lessons I'd give to my stepson was a fifth gift: "confidence in his own talent." I wrote that on a certificate for a course in entrepreneurship for teenagers so he could market the artistic skill so evident in his cartoons.

He really got into it. He gave me concert tickets to Sting and Gloria Estefan, a color printer for my computer and some Laurel Burch earrings, all wrapped in comics from the Sunday paper. His conceptual gift to me was a sign that read "No Speed

Limit!" Besides a white Porsche, Larry gifted me with a vacation in Hawaii, a new PowerBook, a set of Cutco knives and a stud from the pages of Playgirl (for the few times our batteries are out of sync, he wrote). His conceptual gift to me was written on a 3" × 5" card: "I give you the magic sword to conquer your boogie man, permission to be gentle with yourself and license to proceed full steam ahead with the realization of your writing dreams!"

For my beloved, I wrapped up the picture of nose-hair tweezers from a high-end gadget catalog. He got a car, too, a Dodge Viper like the one we saw the weekend we met, plus a leather jacket, more memory for his computer and a video camera so he could practice at his dream career: filmmaker. For his virtual gift, I inscribed a message on a magnifying glass to give him utter and absolute belief in himself and the unlimited power of his creativity. On Christmas morning, looking at his face as he stared out at the sunrise with tears in his eyes, I silently sent him that missing one percent of faith that would help us all actualize our dreams.

The virtual Christmas presents worked. It's amazing how a concept, once put in the mind, can manifest. One year later, we'd moved, and my stepson was registered for a course in art presentation at the local community college. My husband was finishing the college degree he'd stopped working on thirty-one years prior. His belief in himself prompted a midlife career shift to multimedia instructional technology. I'd successfully hoisted that sword to my writing fears, was studying screenwriting and had published some freelance nonfiction.

The three of us found a way to give and love without a worry about costs and returns. I offer it now many years later, with an economy in even deeper trouble than it was back then. I hope our idea helps your family feel the spirit embodied in the man, Jesus, whose birthday we sometimes forget in the rush to shop those few weeks at the end of every year.

We've practiced many a virtual Christmas since then. The bubble of actual gift giving seems to have been permanently burst for us. Perhaps it is time for more of us to let go of the commercialism that underlies this holiday season. I would virtually gift us a view of the human condition that goes beyond one's worth being determined by work, by your job. I'd bless us with divine insight as to how the preciousness of each moment must be cherished. I'd gift us all with the capacity to see the abundance around us everywhere. It is the power of positive intention that counts. Make your holidays this season virtual, and they can still be merry—and much more meaningful!

HUNGRY REINDEER

CHERYL RIVENESS

"Rudolph ate the tree, Mommy! He did, really. Come see. You won't believe it!" the girls clamored around the bed and then jumped in, bouncing, squealing and talking excitedly as five- and seven-year-old girls will do. "Get up! Get up! Hurry!!" By this time, they had wrapped their hands around ours and were dragging us down the hall. We grown-ups played it for all it was worth.

"Girls, come on," their father implored. "What makes you think Rudolph ate our tree?"

"Santa left us a note, Daddy. Look!"

"Hey, babe, look at this." Ed mugged it up, holding out a familiar piece of paper. "It really is a letter from Santa Claus."

"Read it, Mommy, please!" The youngest one looked at me, her huge brown eyes framed by thick lashes. The long dark tresses of her older sister bounced in rhythm to the up and down shaking of her head. How could I not?

"Dear Mimi and Meri," I began. "Thank you so much for the reindeer food. Rudolph and Comet were very hungry, and your tree was just right. I liked the birthday cake, too. Love, Santa."

Presents were forgotten in the moment.

"Mommy, we'll be right back," they yelled as they bounded to the family room door.

"Hey, guys, what about your presents?" I asked, surprised that they were so distracted. "At least change your clothes before you go outside, then you can play until I get breakfast on the table."

They shot each other wide-eyed looks and shrugged their shoulders. "We'll be right back!" they shouted, running down the hall. They were half undressed before they even got to their room.

Five minutes later, they jumped on their red and yellow Huffy bikes and headed down the street. The sun was bright and the sky clear blue with only an occasional fluffy, white cloud. It had been an unusually warm southern California December, and the needles on our tree had turned to brittle tinder in record time. It was the exact kind of tree you hear about bursting into flames every year, and I was not happy about having it there in the living room. But how could I get rid of the Christmas tree before Christmas?

My mother and father were just beginning their snowbird years and had come to spend the holiday season with us. They were as concerned as we were about the potential fire hazard. Mom and I were beginning to get things ready for the morning when she looked at me and asked, "What if Rudolph got hungry tonight?"

Her hazel eyes twinkled in anticipation. Earlier, Dad had gone to the RV where they were staying, but my husband was still up. Grabbing a pruner usually reserved for the Meyer lemon tree, he began at the bottom. We formed a line and got a system going. Snip, pull, hand some cuttings to Mom. Walk it to the living room and hand it off to me to feed it into the fire. It was a relief to see it go. I understood a little better what a fiery inferno feels like and was grateful not to have to worry for another minute.

Once the trunk was fully laid bare, Ed took the strings of lights and wrapped them around it several times. It had begun its life with us as a beautiful fir. Now it was a six-foot knobby stick with illumination.

We had taken artificial snow and left a light dusting from the fireplace to the tree. Using Dad's boots, I managed a few (apparently) believable footprints to add to the illusion. I stuck the note through one of the middle stubs. It looked like something out of a comic strip. We'd have to wait until morning to see if it was believable.

* * *

"Hi, Grandpa. Merry Christmas!" The girls clamored past their grandfather and jumped on their bikes, screaming in delight all the while.

Dad managed to keep the coffee in his cup as he whirled around. "What's going on around here?" He grinned. Laughing, we were filling him in when he raised his cup toward the family window. "Take a look at that."

Turning around, I knew we'd been successful in bringing a small piece of holiday magic into the girls' lives. There were at least a dozen kids of various sizes, all crowded up to the window, hands pressed to the glass, eyes focused on the unbelievable.

MISTLETOE MEMORIES

JEANNE GILPATRICK

*During the holidays, when conversation among friends and cowork-
ers turns to Christmas and favorite memories, I am always reminded,
with a rush of emotion, of my grandson's bittersweet birth.*

* * *

December of 1994, ten days before Christmas, I pulled up in
front of the Florence Crittenton Home for Girls and stared dully
at a string of bright-colored, blinking Christmas lights that framed
a front window. The lights were entirely out of sync with my
heavy mood. The carols, sparkling decor and good cheer of the
holidays seemed like a performance put on for somebody else;
I was in the cheap seats and too far away to catch much of the
show. I was anything but merry. I set my hand brake and steeled
myself against the tears that were one cross look away from spilling.

Once inside, there was nowhere to talk to my daughter, Tara, privately. Her roommate, Rochelle, heavily pregnant, sprawled across the bed on her side of their narrow room and talked on the phone, while her runny-nosed toddler clutched at my pant legs and searched my face for affection. A dozen babies throughout the building cried all at once, and their tired, teenage mothers shouted to one another over the din. Despair seemed to echo through the cold hallways. And so, despite crisp December temperatures, Tara and I headed across the street to sit in my car. I was bundled in a thick jacket and chilled; she was rosy cheeked and toasty in a sleeveless cotton smock and stretchy pants. If she had been older, in a committed relationship or even if this pregnancy had been an accident, I might have teased her about "the little heater" growing inside her. But, it hadn't been an accident. There had been no protection. She had wanted a baby and had ignored my attempts at reason, my pleading and tears. She had refused books outlining the tragic statistics of teen motherhood. At sixteen, she had believed the baby's thirty-year-old, no-account father when he told her he would help her. Abortion? "Out of the question!" she had retorted. Adoption? "How could I?" It was her body. It was her baby, and she wanted it.

And so, too late, perhaps, I had laid down the law: "If you insist on keeping this baby, you cannot live with me." She later confessed that she had thought I would change my mind. But, even as I grew to love the little boy developing inside her, I had stood firm. When she was six months along, I announced that there was a place for her at Florence Crittenton.

I can't remember my heart ever aching more than it did the day I left her there. I prayed that I was doing the right thing. For weeks, I lay awake nights hoping that she would watch the other young mothers' struggles and decide to give her son up for adoption.

But at nine months and two weeks along, as we sat in my car tying sprigs of mistletoe with curly, red ribbon, she remained determined.

She shifted her bulging belly, lifted her chin and threw back her shoulders to give her lungs more room. "Me and Rochelle are going to sell mistletoe on Market Street tomorrow. Rochelle's going to bring her baby. We should get a lot of business, huh? People will look at us and say, 'Poor things,' and give us their money." Her laugh was cut short by one of those "practice" contractions that are common in late pregnancy. She winced and laid her hand on the shelf of her belly as she waited for it to pass. "Whew. I'm getting a lot of those."

"Maybe you're in early labor?"

"Naw."

"Just tuning up, I guess," I said. My heart fluttered momentarily with anticipation of the birth. But the fears that had haunted me since she disclosed her pregnancy were not far away: *She's just a baby herself, single, uneducated. How can she give this child the life he deserves? Only two years earlier, she and her brother climbed trees like children to collect mistletoe to sell in front of our local grocery store.* My chest tightened again, as if in the grip of a giant fist. I had long before given up being angry with her and had committed to making the best of the situation.

"Have you been doing the relaxation exercises?" I asked.

"Sort of." She looked away suddenly, and a heavy silence hung between us. "Rochelle is going to coach me," she blurted at last. My face must have registered this wound. "You said you would be sad and cry, Mom," she explained. "I don't want anybody crying at my baby's birth."

"I said that a long time ago."

"Well, would you?"

"I can't promise that I wouldn't. I love him already. I've told you that. But, it still feels tragic to me." We'd been over it too many times for me to say more. My eyes stung and threatened to spill over. I drew a long breath and gathered my composure. "If you change your mind, you know where to find me." We laughed, and the air was light for just a moment.

"I hope he'll be cute," she said as she zipped a piece of ribbon across the scissors' sharp blade. "I just couldn't stand it if I had an ugly baby." Her words landed like heavy stones, making me weary.

***

Early the next morning, the phone's jingle wrested me from a dream. "This is Mark calling from Florence Crittenton. Tara went into labor this morning, and she's on her way to the hospital."

"Does she want me there?" I asked, my heart racing.

"I don't know. You were just one of the people on her list. We call everybody on the list."

I hung up and dialed the hospital. "Just one of the people on the list" echoed in my head until someone answered.

"My daughter has just been admitted. She's in labor," I heard myself say. It all seemed surreal. Despite the preparation, the therapy, the support group, it still seemed impossible that my baby girl was about to give birth.

"I'll ring her room."

"Hi, Mom. I'm in labor," she chirped. "Are you coming?"

When I arrived, I was alarmed at the commotion in the room. A television hanging from the ceiling was tuned to MTV, full volume, and flashed chaotic images; the phone was ringing; Tara's friend Belinda sat on the hospital bed holding a stuffed, musical bear in a red-and-white Santa's hat. The bear's red nose flashed off and on while it played "Jingle Bells," and Tara and Rochelle stood in the middle of the room convulsed with laughter.

"She peed on the floor," Rochelle screamed.

"I couldn't help it. I was trying to get to the toilet, and it just came too fast," Tara howled, wiping a tear with the back of her hand. She finally composed herself and answered the phone.

Her father. He and his wife, Cheryl, would be there soon. The phone rang again. Tara's friend Natalie this time. Tara promised to let her know as soon as the baby was born.

Belinda seemed determined to keep the "Jingle Bear" wound up in between snapping photos of the nurse, the room and Tara's tremendous belly. "Here, hold the bear and smile, Big Mama. Now, you get in the picture, Rochelle. Smile. Everybody smile!"

Within an hour, though, the contractions had become longer and more intense. Tara turned off the television and asked Belinda to stop winding up the bear. The party was over. She climbed onto the bed and sank into the pillows.

"Want me to rub your back, Big Mama? Want me to massage your feet? Are you hungry or thirsty or anything? You want anything?" Belinda asked, bouncing about the bed.

Tara fluttered one hand like a goodbye gesture, her signal that a contraction was coming, and told Belinda breathlessly, "I want you to go out of the room. I'm sorry. I just want my mom and Rochelle."

Insulted and hurt, Belinda left not only the room but the hospital, too.

"She doesn't understand 'cause she's never had a baby," Rochelle said, gently dabbing at Tara's brow with a damp washcloth.

With the room finally quiet, Tara fell into a predictable rhythm. First, the fluttering hand, a conscious effort to relax, then long deep breaths followed by short pants as she reached the contraction's summit. Once over the top, she sighed, closed her eyes and rested. Rochelle and I, silent and patient, waited on requests for ice chips, juice, a pillow adjustment, a back massage.

Then, suddenly, Cheryl exploded into the room with Tara's father, Brad, hanging uncertainly in the doorway. Her very presence was like screeching chalk. She hugged and kissed, consoled and laid presents on Tara right through a contraction.

Like a marathoner reaching for the strength to cross a finish line, Tara struggled to muster a smile. "Thanks, thanks," she said, setting the presents unopened on her bedside table. Tara's father excused himself while Cheryl made herself at home in a rocking chair and began to chatter. Tara's eyes implored me as her belly began to tighten again. As this contraction gathered strength, it alarmed her. Her eyes grew wide, and she let out a moan before it was over. Her eyes begged me. "Mom, I don't want everybody seeing me in pain," she whispered. "Please tell Cheryl to go." I did. Then she turned to her friend. "I'm sorry, Rochelle. I only want my mom here now."

When the nurse determined that Tara was dilated to six centimeters, she suggested that a warm bath might be comforting.

I watched her, lying on her side, naked in the bath with her knees pulled up under her great belly, and I marveled at how she had once floated like this inside of me.

Her eyes were closed now, rolled back deep. Tiny beads of perspiration glistened on her forehead. Her breathing was quiet and shallow as she rested between contractions. She opened her eyes and tightened her grasp on my hand. Our eyes locked, and we breathed together, long, deep breaths. Her grip grew stronger and more urgent as she climbed the contraction's arc. We panted. Reached the top. And her hand relaxed in mine as she slid down the other side. Watching her, breathing with her, feeling her contractions through the squeeze of her hand, I was transported along with her into a timeless, spaceless dimension. The fixtures in the room were fluid. The floor, the walls, the ceiling breathed with us, throbbed along with our pulses. There was no one in the world now but us—two women working together to give birth to a baby.

"Mom," Tara whispered. I leaned close. "This is so hard."

"I know," I said. "I know."

* * *

Nine centimeters. The nurse went out to find the midwife. The contractions were intense and close together now. "Why does this have to hurt so much?" Tara implored.

"You're almost there, Tara," the midwife cooed as she entered the room and pulled on exam gloves. "Ten centimeters! You can push as soon as you feel the urge." Instinctively, Tara hoisted herself from her back onto her hands and knees and beared down. Three long grunts, and the crown of his dark, wet head was visible. My heart danced. "Push hard!" the midwife commanded. Tara screamed and pushed out his shoulders.

"Oh, my God!" I said.

One last, great push, and he was out.

I was breathless as I watched the midwife place him on his mother's deflated belly, riveted by this tiny, perfect person, his umbilical cord still throbbing. "My God," I heard myself say again and again. His eyes blinked slowly and reflected the kind of wisdom I have seen in the eyes of very old people who seem at peace, ready anytime to go to their God. For just an instant, I was certain that he had come to us from God, and my heart, suddenly filled with hope, seemed too big for my body.

My eyes and heart followed him as the nurse took him to a metal table to be weighed, measured and tested. His mouth turned down at the corners as she jabbed and jostled him, and his chin began to tremble violently. Suddenly, he let out a wail that resonated through every cell of me, and I yearned to snatch him from the nurse and comfort him. I wanted to wrap him in something warm, rock him and hold him close to my heart. He was so tiny in her hands, naked and vulnerable. His life depends entirely on us, I thought, and my chin began to tremble, too. "My God, forgive us," I said to myself, and I turned my back to my daughter so she wouldn't see my tears.

***

Nine days later, a tiny Santa in a shiny red suit trimmed in fluffy white at the collar and cuffs lay sleeping on a soft blanket beneath my Christmas tree.

***

My daughter is 34 years old now, and my grandson is 17. She has raised him mostly on her own, with financial help from me and various agencies. It has not been easy, nor ideal, and they have their struggles. Every Christmas season, though, the sight of mistletoe, just like hearing a familiar song, brings back a crystal clear memory of my grandson's birth, and I am reminded of the amazing gift that he is.

MR. CHRISTMAS

RUTH ANDREW

After my marriage of twenty-three years ended and we divvied up the family ornaments, I hated the thought of putting up a Christmas tree.

Divorced, living in an apartment alone in Spokane, Washington, with an all-consuming marketing job, Christmas had become a lonely time for me. I wondered what other divorced women did for the holidays, after their families had moved on with their own lives. Of course, there were the usual Christmas lunches, office parties and gift exchanges, the hurry and scurry of Christmas cards and last-minute fudge making. For the first time ever, I bought Christmas cookies at the grocery store. The only thing that saved even a little bit of holiday spirit for me was going to church for the lighting of the Advent candles and the Christmas hymns. There was no joy left in giving gifts to friends, baking Christmas cookies and decorating the family tree.

A nice, red poinsettia on the dining room table was the most I could get into the spirit of the holiday. I still enjoyed the Christmas cards, but I also found that many of our married friends no longer kept in touch. I didn't understand this. I could still enjoy their holiday letters and photos, even if I no longer wore a wedding ring. How could this happen? We'd always been good friends. I felt left out and alone.

Each year leading up to Christmas, I dreaded the holidays with a vengeance. It would start in October, around Halloween, and dominate Thanksgiving for me. By December, I always felt like Scrooge. One particular Christmas was worse than the others. My son, Phil, a college student, met and fell in love with Diane, the beautiful young woman he would later marry, and spent Christmas with her family in Mt. Vernon, Washington. This same Christmas, my daughter, Allison, was in France for her junior year in high school as a World Experience exchange student. I was alone for the holidays.

And then, during this most lonely of all Christmas seasons, I met Mr. Christmas himself. He smiled at me whenever we passed each other in the building where we both worked. One chilly morning, he stopped by my desk, handed me a cup of coffee and invited me to lunch that afternoon. His name was Dennis, and we married on November 25 of the following year. Then, our holiday problems began. Dennis loved Christmas, wanted a big Christmas tree and wanted it early. I hated the thought and insisted that a poinsettia on the dining room table was enough. By this time, I reasoned, we were empty nesters. We did not need a Christmas tree, and the poinsettia would do. But he insisted on a tree. The first year, I actually won the battle, and instead of a tree, we hung a cedar swag over the family room entertainment center.

After a few days, I began to notice ornaments adorning the swag, and they looked eerily familiar. Then, more ornaments appeared on the swag. Each day, after coming home from work, I'd check the swag, convinced that it held more ornaments than the day before. After a week, every ornament stored downstairs in boxes found their way to our Christmas tree swag, as Dennis called it. When I'd adjusted to this, I walked into our family room one evening to find him stringing twinkling lights around the swag.

From then on, for the next twenty-something years, it was the same issue: have a tree or not have a tree. He always won. At least I nixed a real tree with needles falling all over the carpet. Dennis bought a reasonable-size artificial tree. He put it up, and he took it down. You'd think I'd have gotten over it in time, but years later I still wanted no part of a Christmas tree. And besides, I reasoned, it only affected me once a year.

Last year in November, just before Thanksgiving, I e-mailed my good friend Gail, whom I'd known for years, and bemoaned that Dennis was talking about Christmas and I was dreading it all over again. I described the sad evening my children's father and I sat in the downstairs of our family home to divide up our Christmas ornaments, before the divorce was actually final. He got the Raggedy Andy ornament. I got the Raggedy Ann. He got the furry lion ornament. I took Mrs. Claus. And so it went until our twenty-three years of collected family ornaments were divided, including ornaments from Gail and her husband when they were in Germany with the Air Force.

And now, all these years later, our family still didn't gather to decorate the tree. Each December, it seemed like we weren't a family anymore, and I could hardly look at our ornaments without a deep sadness sweeping over me. Sitting in my home office that afternoon, sipping a glass of Merlot, I read Gail's return e-mail. She scolded me soundly. "It's time you get over this," she wrote. "Why would you let your ex-husband steal your Christmas joy? Dennis loves Christmas, and he loves a tree. He must feel horrible every year when you act like this."

I thanked her for her wisdom and knew she'd spoken from the heart. I felt consumed by guilt, realizing I'd deprived Dennis of his own Christmas joy the way I thought my ex-husband had stolen mine. In reality, I'd done it to myself. This had gone on long enough!

That evening, as Dennis and I ate dinner, I asked him quietly if he would mind getting out the tree for Christmas. He was stunned.

"Really?" he asked. "You mean it?"

"Yes."

"Even before Thanksgiving?"

"Yes. Absolutely. Tonight!"

I gave him a kiss and explained my change of heart. "Gail told me this afternoon that I should not let my ex-husband steal all of my Christmas joy any longer and that I had been unfair to you all these years, when you love it so much. I've decided she's right. Now I want to enjoy every minute of Christmas with you."

"Great!" he exclaimed.

I smiled. "From now on, I'd like to put our tree up in late November, before our anniversary on the 25th. We can call it our anniversary tree, if you like."

He kissed me, then hurried downstairs and returned with our tree, already decorated with the ornaments and lights from the previous year. Getting me to put ornaments on it the last year was such an issue for me that he left it decorated and threw a sheet over it in the downstairs storage closet. He told me he never wanted to go through that hassle again, and neither did I, for that matter. It turned out to be a blessing. In a mere ten minutes, our beautiful anniversary tree was ablaze in the living room with twinkling lights, ornaments and love.

This tree held my family ornaments, and I felt only joy remembering the ones my son and daughter had given me, treasures from long ago. Phil and Diane had given me a beautiful

White House Christmas ornament from when they were first married and living in Maryland, as well as sweet ornaments from their children, my darling granddaughters, Jamie and Tate. I found five red-and-white candy canes that Allison had made when she was only five years old in kindergarten, when she was the same age as her small son, Asher, himself in kindergarten last December. I found the bread dough sheep from Phil's Cub Scout days, which he'd always insisted he didn't make, but his name was still printed on the back. And I found the white star Allison had made in preschool, with the pink ball fringe in the middle.

Standing in my living room surrounded by ornaments from my children when they were small, I understood how much I'd missed our family Christmas tree. We were still a family. That was the important thing. I felt like rolling up my sleeves and baking a big batch of Christmas cookies.

The more I looked at our tree, the more I realized how many ornaments my husband had collected from family and friends over our years together. A moose looked at me from beneath a branch on the tree. I found a small computer, several kayaks, a Santa in a canoe and many others that spoke to my husband's job in manufacturing and also his love of kayaks, canoes and the outdoors.

Later that evening, Dennis and I sat on the living room sofa with the lights out in the room except for those twinkling on the tree. I marveled at the beauty of our tree before us, the love it represented, and wondered how I'd ever allowed myself to be too sad to want a Christmas tree, especially when my husband loved one so much.

I sat there long after Dennis had kissed me goodnight and gone to bed. When I finally turned out the tree lights, I found myself quietly singing and humming a bit of "Santa Baby" as I headed off to bed myself, eager to get up early the next morning to turn on the tree lights for breakfast. I wanted to be up early and bake those Christmas cookies, even if it was before Thanksgiving. I smiled to myself, knowing my lemon sugar cookie recipe was from Gail, when we were both new brides so many years earlier.

This year, I was the one who reminded Dennis in late November that it was time to get out the Christmas tree, even before the Thanksgiving turkey was to go into the oven. And that's the way it is at our house now, thanks to a very good friend with a whole lot of wisdom, and a husband who always understood.

IS THIS A GOOD TIME?

RUTH CAMPBELL BREMER

Cradling a sleeping baby in one arm, I was trying to throw together an afternoon snack without tripping on the dogs when my phone rang. It was my husband, Alex. "Is it okay if I invite a couple guys over for dinner?" he asked.

I hesitated, scanning the messy kitchen and cluttered countertops. This was our first year hosting Christmas, and I had this idea that it should be picture-perfect, complete with handmade decorations and a big holiday feast. My attempt at personalized Christmas stockings had resulted in a glitter paint disaster, and I'd run out of time to do anything else crafty. The living room furniture had been awkwardly rearranged to accommodate our hand-me-down artificial tree, decorated with unbreakable ornaments near the bottom.

Picture-perfect it was not. After more than a year of renovating our house, it was still a gallery of unfinished projects. A section of cabinets remained unpainted, face plates were missing from light switches and outlets, and the fixtures were mismatched and outdated. The refrigerator was decorated with fingerprints and magnetic letters, and various objects were stacked on top in a most unattractive fashion. In one corner, a large potted plant was dying a slow death.

"Sure," I told Alex, trying to sound enthusiastic. "The more the merrier." My parents had just arrived, and to be honest, it didn't feel like an especially good time to have additional company. Still, I couldn't bring myself to say no. After all, it was the day before Christmas Eve, and these poor guys were stuck in Denver when they were supposed to be at home enjoying the holiday break with their families.

A few days earlier, a blizzard had dumped two feet of snow on the area, closing the airport for forty-five hours and causing power outages, road closures and shortages at local grocery stores. People were gradually digging out and getting back to work, but there were piles of snow everywhere, driving was still a little sketchy and the airport had a backlog of flights trying to get out of town.

For some reason, Alex's company had chosen the week before Christmas to bring in a group of salespeople from around the country for training. Everyone else had managed to secure a flight home already. These two guys, however, were stuck in town for one more night. Although they each had a nice room at the Hyatt and an expense account to cover dinner, Alex thought they might prefer to hang out with a family instead of spending the evening alone.

Just as I got off the phone, my two-month-old daughter woke up and started screaming in my ear. No, it definitely was not a good time to have people over. Fortunately, my mom was there to help. She started peeling potatoes and planning the dinner menu while I fed the baby. Then, we got to work clearing off the dining room table. Even in my slightly panicked state, I felt excitement bubbling up at the thought of gathering a crowd around our table. This was my opportunity to host a big Christmas dinner. So what if it wouldn't be anywhere near perfect?

For years, Alex and I had lived in small houses and condos. With space tight and our budget even tighter, we ate dinner off whatever hand-me-down or cheap, prefabricated table we could squeeze into the available dining area. Then we were finally able to buy our own home: a 1960s two-story with scuffed-up hardwood and drafty, single-pane windows. One of our favorite features was the dining room. Taking up a quarter of the main floor, it was big enough to hold a real dining table. And for the first time, we could afford to buy one.

When we brought home the large, sturdy, solid wood table, I could already picture us enjoying it in the decades to come. Oh, the plans I had for that dining table. It would be the centerpiece for holidays, family gatherings, celebrations and impromptu dinners with friends. We would start eating dinner as a family every night, complete with meaningful, stimulating conversation. I could host play dates and bunco night, throw intimate dinner parties and large rowdy gatherings. Having a real dining room with a real dining table was going to transform our very lives.

Then, reality interfered. Once the table and chairs were set up in the dining room, we managed maybe two or three chaotic family dinners before proceeding to gradually cover the table with stuff. Since the dining room was located immediately to the right of the front door and directly on the path to the kitchen, one half of the table became a landing pad for junk mail, canned food, arts and crafts projects, assorted papers and all kinds of homeless items. The other end was where we ate (rarely all together), and it usually held a few dirty dishes from the latest meal.

Somehow, the festive gatherings I'd always imagined taking place around the table still hadn't materialized. Between keeping up with two little boys, a draining pregnancy followed by the utter exhaustion of caring for a newborn, I never seemed to have the time or energy to complete even the simplest home improvement projects. I was always in a foggy-headed survival mode, with toys scattered everywhere, dirty dishes in the sink and the boys making messes faster than I could clean them up. It was just never a good time to have people over.

Well, I guess this is just going to have to be a good time, I thought as Mom and I cleared the papers and junk off the table. I would never have planned a big dinner on this particular night. But then again, maybe I never would have planned it at all. When was I ever going to decide it was a good time? When the house was completely fixed up and sparkling clean? When we had nothing on the schedule and nothing stressful going on in our lives? It hit me that it would never truly be a good time. But ultimately, what that meant was, any time could be a good time.

As the sun set and the temperature dropped outside, our house came alive with holiday music, noise and voices. My brother Jeff lived in Denver at the time, and he came over with his girlfriend, Danielle. Alex arrived a bit later with the two visiting salesmen, Lamar and DJ. They were in high spirits after a narrow escape from the snow-covered office parking lot and a slow drive home on slick roads.

Sure enough, it was a good time. No, it was a *great* time. As darkness fell outside and the bitter cold settled in for the night, our home was transformed into a safe haven of light and warmth. When I glanced into the living room, the string of lights on the Christmas tree seemed to glow a little brighter. Mom had dinner going, and the delicious aromas filled the house. Alex opened a bottle of wine. Danielle held the baby while Jeff wrestled with my two-year-old son. Dad and Lamar chatted about the snow-storm, and DJ was locked in a deep discussion with my four-year-old about the existence of Santa Claus and Pluto's recent demotion to dwarf planet.

When the food was ready, we pulled more chairs around the table, poured some more wine and sat down to enjoy our humble feast in the company of new friends. Everyone shared stories, jokes and laughter. Lamar and DJ were successful financial wholesalers with generous expense accounts. They were used to the best of the best, regularly taking clients out to trendy restaurants and drinking expensive wine. They could have eaten steak or lobster that night, yet they both seemed genuinely grateful to spend the evening sitting down to a home-cooked meal with us instead.

* * *

Because of the sleep deprivation that accompanies a new baby, I don't remember a whole lot from that period in my life, but I will never forget that evening. I can't recall what we ate or what kind of wine we drank with our holiday meal. What I remember is the warmth, the laughter and the bonding taking place around that big table. I was overcome with joy at having the opportunity to finally use the table exactly the way I'd always wanted. But I also realized something deeper. It wasn't the table. I could have been experiencing this all along, around any table, in any kind of living space. That night, nobody noticed or cared if there were face plates on the light switches, dust in the corners or abstract art on the stockings. I was experiencing perfection in spite of the messy, imperfect setting.

For me, the warm glow continued through the holiday season. It was wonderful having my family there, reveling in the kids' excitement and snuggling with the new baby. I don't remember any of the presents I gave or received that Christmas. I only remember one perfect gift that came in the form of a blizzard: the realization that there will never really be a good time. My life will never be tidy and organized, and my house will never look like a scene from a Pottery Barn catalog. A good time to get together with friends, family or complete strangers is right now.

In the years since, we've moved to other houses in other cities, and life has not slowed down one bit. I still haven't managed to get everything in order or keep my house clean for more than two minutes. Not once have we hosted a picture-perfect Christmas. Now I just count myself lucky if nobody comes down with the flu during the holiday break. I've come to terms with the fact that laundry and dishes are never really done. Now, with three big kids and all their activities and projects, our house is still messy, our schedule is busier than ever, and most of our friends seem to be in a time crunch, too.

Sometimes I still find myself thinking it's not a good time to invite people over. But when I look at our big, sturdy dining table (which is typically covered in crayons, construction paper, Lego bricks and dirty dishes), I'm reminded of the Christmas gift I received on that snowy night in Denver, and I know the truth.

FIRST FAMILY CHRISTMAS

JACK SKILLICORN

It was sixty days before Christmas, and all were apart. I had just re-enlisted in the Air Force and was stationed in Massachusetts. I was engaged to a wonderful woman, Sandy, who came complete with a small daughter, Jeanette. My family-to-be was at home in California. Since Christmas was fast approaching and our telephone calls were getting longer and more expensive, I knew it was time for me to head west. With a wedding, I would make my family-to-be officially my family, and the three of us would head back east to start our new home together.

I found us a place to live. I got permission to head back for a few days, and soon we were in the happy midst of a small family wedding ceremony. We were joined by my mother, the bride's five-year-old daughter, her mother and father and the minister at the Los Altos United Methodist Church.

After the wedding, my wife and I, along with our daughter and my mother, checked in to a marvelous hotel. With its gardens, fountains and statuary, it was a magnificent wonder in the eyes of a five-year-old. Even more wonderful to a five-year-old was the announcement I made at the dinner table.

"Jeanette, this is a very special occasion. Our first dinner together as a family. You can order anything you want from the menu. Anything at all."

She studied the menu carefully. "Anything?"

"Yes, that's right. Anything you want."

She sat up and put the menu on the table next to her fork. "All right, I want cheesecake."

"Cheesecake? Is that all?" Her mother and I exchanged quick smiles.

"I want my cheesecake first, that's what I want." Well, she had us there, anything she wanted meant just that. Our waitress was upset by the idea. She had never seen it done before, so it must not be healthy, and she told us so, in no uncertain terms. Years later, whenever we bring up that first meal together, Jeanette does not remember anything else she had, but she sure remembers the day she got to eat her dessert first.

The next morning after breakfast, we said farewell to my mother and our cross-country adventure began.

For our trip, we had purchased a brand-new 1962 Nash Rambler station wagon. We had carefully planned our trip to be a relaxed drive on Highway 80, approximately 3,200 miles. The plan was to drive six hours each day, not including whatever stops we made. While we drove east, our furniture and other items, including our daughter's Christmas gifts, were being transported by a moving van. We knew we were cutting it close, but the van was scheduled to arrive two days before Christmas.

What a feeling. Christmas in the air, the magnificent Sierra Nevada mountains as a backdrop to our first day of driving across the country. A couple of small bears playing at the side of the road gave Jeanette a thrill almost as big as the cheesecake, as did the discovery of free Howard Johnson children's coloring books. Every morning at breakfast, we sought out a Howard Johnson restaurant, and she would carefully fill in the same pictures she'd done the day before.

Over the following days, we stopped in many states, cities and villages, seeing many interesting places and sights. But in between our stops, we played games, like who could recognize the most license plates from different states or the alphabet game, where you find letters on signs along the road. To keep Jeanette in the proper holiday frame of mind, we sang whatever Christmas songs came to mind, such as "Away in a Manger" and "Santa Claus Is Coming to Town." Our voices might not have been professional, but to me the sound of our three voices struggling to hit the notes and remember the words was better than anything on the radio dial.

We had lucked out with the weather, and it was beautifully clear for the first few days. Getting toward Illinois, we began to notice dark clouds overhead. I turned on the radio. According to the reports, it was a big storm indeed, and it sounded like it would be moving in lock step with us as we headed back east.

"Do you think this is going to delay our moving van?" my wife asked quietly, not wanting Jeanette to hear.

"I don't know," I said, glancing up at the sky. "I hope not. Everything we have is in that van, including her presents. I would hate for her to wake up Christmas morning in a new town, in a new house, and find nothing under the tree."

Finally, there we were, and I was pulling the Nash into our own driveway. I borrowed some furniture from the squadron where I worked, to use until our furniture arrived and we moved in.

"We need a tree," my wife said, looking at the mismatched furniture scattered around the living room. "The ornaments are all in the moving boxes. We should have brought a few in the car with us. Well, we can make them this year." And make them we did, the three of us. We bought cranberries, popped popcorn, and Jeanette and I sat on the floor, stringing beautiful red-and-white garlands for our tree. We wrapped our colorful, homemade garland around and through the evergreen branches of our tree. Now, really in the Christmas spirit, we decided the tree needed something more. We found some apples, ribbon and cardboard and made our own hanging ornaments. Shiny stars dangled among the branches, and a larger, glorious star was at the top of the tree. It may not have been the fanciest tree in the neighborhood, but it was OUR tree.

Therefore, for us, it was the best tree anywhere.

The van had been scheduled to arrive on December 22, but where was it? My wife and I whispered about it, and she made more than one call to the company headquarters to hear their apologetic reports of a truck in the midst of severe weather. We hope Jeanette wouldn't notice our concern. But she did.

"Santa, will you be able to find my new house on Christmas Eve? We just moved here," we heard her explain to a Santa in a local shopping mall.

He smiled and reassured her, bless his heart. "Of course, dear. I can find everyone on Christmas Eve."

Could he really? On December 24, the moving van was already two days late from the last promised arrival day. We were sitting around the tree, anxiously waiting to see the moving van come rumbling up our street, when the phone rang.

"It's our driver," my wife whispered, covering the phone with her hand. "He's asking if he can stop at his sister's house for Christmas Eve!" I sighed and shook my head. "Can you please try to make it," she asked him. "All of our presents are in that truck." She listened quietly to his response. "He'll do the best he can," she told me, hanging up the phone.

Jeanette went to bed early that night, dreaming of Santa's visit. Her parents, however, were too nervous to do anything other than pace in front of the window, pulling the curtain back regularly and holding their breath every time headlights turned onto the street. Finally, at ten o'clock on Christmas Eve, weeks after we had loaded our cardboard boxes into a moving van, a pair of headlights pulled into our driveway.

Jeanette crept down the stairs in the morning. Arms around each other's waists, we watched as she caught her first glimpse of the living room.

"He did it! Santa did it!" she shouted as she sat among the many packages by the Christmas tree. "He found our new house!" She hugged an enormous stuffed puppy to her chest—it was almost bigger than she was. Yes, Santa finally came, spreading gifts under the tree, filling her Christmas stocking and giving this brand-new family a holiday to remember.

LIPSTICK CHRISTMAS

INGRID E. LUNDQUIST

Sue and I met in 1975, and every December we provide each other with moral support and the nod of approval when selecting Christmas gifts for our sisters, brothers, parents, boyfriends and husbands. This year, she arrived at my office wearing broken-in jeans, a denim shirt and a burnt-orange rain jacket that had seen several wet winters. Tall and thin, Sue looked like she was making a denim-casual fashion statement. I, however, was average height with extra pounds. I was dressed in similar denim, but my look was of someone who grabbed the first clothes she could find, newly warm from the dryer.

We'd both become comfortable with dressing casually, unlike our dating years when we slipped our callous-free feet into red, ankle-strapped stilettos, pulled on short saucy outfits, kept a full palette of nail colors in our refrigerator vegetable bins and wore lacy underwear. In our younger days, we always painted our lips.

"Forget your lipstick?" she asked, looking at my pale face.

"Yeah," I said, with the enthusiasm of opening a utility bill. "I guess," I added, as if my response required more than just acknowledgment. Maybe with the passing of time, we had forgotten or perhaps just didn't care anymore about being stylish.

Our lives had certainly changed since we'd met back in college, but there was one constant: our mutual lack of holiday spirit. Instead of looking forward to the retail-promised jingle bell cheer, Sue and I both dreaded the holiday season. This was just another dreary, rainy Thursday in December. On our gift lists, we both had a family member who requested a leaf blower. The year was 1999, fondly remembered as the leaf blower Christmas.

Sue and I were our fathers' sons. We owned power tools and knew every aisle in every hardware store in town. There was a leaf blower sale at a hardware store close to my office. We went there, and it was an easy three-minute purchase, so we wasted another ten minutes groveling through the bargain bins to stock up on tape measures, screwdrivers and night lights.

In the parking lot, we inhaled the memory-laden smell of steamed hot dogs. "When you were a kid, did your dad take you to the hardware store on Saturday mornings?" she asked.

"We usually went to Sears," I said grinning. "They had fresh popcorn with real butter by the paint section."

On the drive back to my office, I noticed empty parking spaces in front of a local bar. "Let's stop and see if it's still the same," I said, pulling into a space and not waiting for Sue to reply.

The Palomino Room was an old-time hangout, aptly named for attracting male patrons primarily over the age of sixty-five. We had both just turned fifty-two. The place hadn't changed with the times. There was still the dark wainscot paneling and blue fleur-de-lis wallpaper with an occasional stain of men's hair cream. "Hey, look," I said, pointing to the starched, white table linens. "I bet those apricot-colored napkins have been folded a million times into swans."

Today's diners were holiday shoppers or older children with their elderly parents, who gummed soft white rolls and chicken rice soup. Some were savoring the signature dessert, chocolate mousse with a generous dollop of whipped cream, served in a glass, soda fountain–style ice cream dish.

The bar area was empty. The cracked red leather on the stools seemed more inviting than the corner alcove. It was always dark here, a place where secrets are kept. Dark and close like a cave. This was the place married men took their girlfriends.

The bar was quite a distance from the main door. We mounted two stools and settled in. We had a good vantage point from which to survey the crowd. The bar menu featured New England clam chowder served with soda crackers—a perfect winter accompaniment. Soup it was.

"Can I get a white roll and butter?" Sue asked the bartender.

"Tabasco sauce for me," I noted.

Over bowls of thick, creamy soup, we were content, eating, talking about Christmas plans and sketching holiday table decor ideas on paper cocktail napkins.

The rain pelted the sidewalk, splashing up against the swinging door, but the sky occasionally pushed through a ribbon of afternoon light. The door swung open and closed several times without incident. Then, a temporary blinding wedge of light shot across the empty cocktail tables in front of the bar. A man and woman snaked their way to the bar and sat down. *Hmmm, wonder what the story was there . . .*

"They're not married," I whispered to Sue.

"At least not to each other," she whispered back.

He wore a well-tailored, indigo banker's suit with a Santa tie, and she looked like an elongated, pink cotton ball in a straight skirt and matching fuzzy sweater. The intimate bar area now felt inhabited, and everyone was talking so loudly about nothing that eavesdropping was impossible.

Another streak of light ushered in two more silhouettes. This time, the hinged door swung shut slowly, leaving a sunlit haze and making it difficult to see. I studied the incomplete outlines as my mind melded a hodgepodge image, forming a recognizable shape I could only define as male.

"They look like lumberjacks," I said to Sue.

"After a hard day's work," she replied.

Okay, we were wearing faded and casual denim, but these guys looked downright scruffy. They wore wet jackets, maybe plaid or fatigue style, and both had shaggy beards. From their rugged appearance, I grimaced as I instinctively knew they smelled of something unpleasant. I was glad the nicely dressed man and fuzzy woman served as a shield between us and them.

The men's movement through the door was at first swift but came to an abrupt stop. I looked closer at the back-lit men, trying to determine whether we were in danger. "Are they going to hold up the restaurant and take us hostage," I asked beneath my breath, "or kidnap us, tape our mouths and drag us off to their shabby, pungent pickup truck?"

My eyes focused on the figures while thoughts raced through my mind as if preparing to give the police a description for a lineup. The taller one had familiar eyes—no, he had familiar something else. It was his size that was familiar. I noticed he must have been 6'4" or 6'5" as he ducked under the doorjamb. Sue was looking at the other man. He was shorter, probably about 6'. He didn't catch my attention at all.

"The tall one is staring at me," I either said, or thought I said, as I tried not to stare. He'd walk a pace or two forward, then stop and stare, then walk another pace forward, and stop and stare. I was uncomfortable and shifted my attention to my soup.

I guess the shorter one was looking at Sue. Her stiff body language indicated she was scared, too. "Ingrid . . . don't those guys look familiar?" she asked.

I glanced at the shorter one and responded bluntly, "No." I was really afraid and forced my eyes back to the chowder, all the while trying to imagine how I would react if they pulled a gun and wondering if I had anything of value in my purse to offer them in trade for my life.

I sneaked another peek at the taller one as he continued to walk closer. I focused. I focused harder. I literally felt my head tilt as if to question whether I was really seeing what I thought I was seeing. My memory collided with the man before me. Now I was staring into his stare, eyeball to eyeball. I became anxious. My face flushed more quickly than it had since junior prom, when my date touched my nylon stocking–encased thigh. My heart thumped like a train on old tracks, picking up speed down a snowy mountain.

Our eyes made direct, close contact. "Look familiar?" I yelped, leaping into his now outstretched arms. "Sue, it's your ex-husband!" Sue couldn't hear me, crushed as she was in a warm embrace with my ex-boyfriend.

Don and Herb. Some thirty years before, Sue had been married to Don, and I had been head over heels in love with Herb. Both moved out of town shortly after college but returned each Christmas to visit families. That day, they were buying last-minute gifts for their wives and kids. For the afternoon, it felt like old times. We were happy, the four of us, laughing, hugging and reminiscing.

Since then, Sue and I make it a point to go Christmas shopping wearing proper clothes and makeup. You just never know who might turn up in your life.

When we recall the excitement on the faces of our loved ones when they opened the leaf blowers, we're primed to meet the ghosts of Christmas past. But nearing 40 years now, it's become evident that our annual treks during the holidays are not about shopping at all. No? No, it is actually about the bond we've formed by adding yet another unbelievable story to yet another year of friendship. It's our holiday tradition.

ENOUGH TIME FOR CHRISTMAS

JULAINA KLEIST-CORWIN

Every year, I groan when I think about sorting through all the Christmas decorations, the time it takes to decorate, and then a few weeks later, to pack it up again. What makes it all worthwhile is a crumpled and now yellowed piece of newsprint, a story that my son, Adrian, wrote for a newspaper contest. I keep it in the storage box to reread each season. A few years after he wrote it, he passed away from an accident.

***

I don't have any specific memories of Christmas because they have blurred together over the years. I don't see Christmas as a celebration of a religious leader's birthday mainly because I'm not a religious person. I see it as a time of happiness and good feelings. A time when relatives come over, a time of giving things, pine needles and presents. I can remember things that happened on Christmas, but I can't accurately remember when they happened, if it was last year or the year before or the year before that.

I remember my father buying a tall tree and trying to make it stand up straight in the stupid and poorly designed stand. I remember him stringing the tree lights and wondering if we needed an extra set. We always needed another set.

I remember hanging the ornaments, the gold and blue shining ones, the old, fragile ones that came from my great-grandmother. The dorky ones I made out of paper plates and Shrinky Dinks in second grade, the reindeer from clothespins and the heavy ones made from plaster molds that could only be hung on the low, thick branches. The gaudy tinsel strings that are always spread around the house for lack of a better place to put them. Now my dad hangs the ornaments about a week before Christmas. We don't seem to have much time anymore.

I remember Grandma toting presents and her hugs and kisses. I remember the presents, the bow and arrow, the space men and Legos, the shirts and socks, the plastic Creepy Crawlers set, the bag of doohickeys and thingamajigs, the model sets, the electric trains and toy cars, the abundant supply of aftershave for Dad and Grandpa and the never-enough See's chocolates.

I remember the box of presents from the relatives in Wisconsin. The undersized box would burst and spew unknown gifts. My mother would always open them before Christmas. She said she was just checking to see if she bought the same thing so she could take it back in time to get something different. I knew she just wanted to see her presents early.

I remember the Christmases in the mountains at the rented cabin. We would lug the suitcases, presents, skis, car chains and the miniature, plastic tree, complete with lights and ornaments that Grandma brought. We don't go up to the cabin anymore. We just don't seem to have the time.

But the thing I remember the most is the lights. The glowing tree lights in the windows of the houses down the street, the flashing lights tracing the edges of the roofs. The giant tree of lights on the top of the Concord Park and Shop sign. I made a habit the last couple Christmas seasons to look out the front window right before I go to bed. With the house lights off, I can see the lights from the other houses far down the street. I see the lights glowing and flashing their message of Christmas.

As I grow older, I seem to lose the time to enjoy Christmas like I used to. I just hope I always have enough time to recall my Christmas memories.

***

Who knew that he wouldn't have enough time for more Christmas memories, not enough time to enjoy future holidays? I hear

Adrian's voice clearly when I read his story, I see the scenes he describes. I feel the childhood memories as if they were yesterday, bringing him close to me again.

FOGGY DAY

LOUISE REARDON

It was not the best of Christmas seasons that year, 1944. As I rode down through California's Central Valley on the train on December 23, I had plenty of time to think about my husband, Ed, in the Air Force, loading bombs onto planes at the Battle of the Bulge. Although he had been diligent about writing two or three times a week, it had been weeks since I'd last heard from him. I dreaded the news that might be slowly winding its way toward me.

The usually dependable Southern Pacific train was anything but dependable during wartime. As the hours wore on, I realized that although the schedule called for the train to arrive in Tulare at 11:00 p.m., we were not going to arrive at 11:00 or 12:00 or even at 1:00 a.m. Finally, at 3:00 in the morning, the train pulled into the station. The depot had long since closed for the night, and I looked anxiously around for signs that someone had come to meet me. As a schoolteacher living up north in Sacramento, I made this train trip home quite regularly, and my folks always came to the station to pick me up. But that morning, there was no sign of them.

"Louise!" I heard someone calling my name from the parking lot. Peering out into the thick tule fog peculiar to the valley, I could make out a lone car. To my surprise, I saw that it was not my parents emerging from the fog but two old pals from high school who had been sitting there in the cold and dark for hours waiting for my train to arrive. They were tired and worn out, not only from the long wait but also from the yearly ritual that orange growers undergo in cold weather to keep their trees from freezing—lighting smudge pots in the orchards to create a low, heavy smoke to keep the warmth close to the ground. Growers' children would sometimes drag into school in the morning with rings under their eyes from smudging all night and black streaks on their faces from the oily smoke.

I was overjoyed to see them, but I wondered where my parents were. As we drove through the countryside toward my hometown of Strathmore, they filled me in on my family's news: My grandmother had broken her hip and was in the hospital. My sister Barbara, due to give birth to her first child, was in the same hospital with what appeared to be serious complications with her baby. An X-ray showed a breech baby with an abnormally large head. The doctor feared the worst. My father had been close to a breakdown and was lying in bed with worry.

I added this distressing information to the worry I already had about my husband. I thanked my friends for the ride and went into the house to see what I could do to help. I found my sister's best friend close to hysterics. Like mine, her husband was also at the Battle of the Bulge. He was a doctor stationed at Nancy, and she had not heard from him in weeks either. But the immediate problem at hand was to track down Barbara's husband, Giz, to tell him the latest development with his wife's pregnancy. The two of us turned our attention from worrying about our own husbands to worrying about Barbara's. He was a B-24 pilot scheduled to head out to fight in the Pacific, and we found that he was currently only three hundred miles to the north of us, on an air base in San Francisco. His commanding officer told us that he was on alert status and ready to be shipped out to the Pacific at any time. He would not be able to attend the birth.

December 24 passed slowly. We went back and forth to the hospital all day long, listening all the while to the terrifying news on the radio about the fight raging in Europe. As the day wore on, we were told that the doctors did not want to delay Barbara's delivery any longer and that they planned to do a cesarean. Good news arrived when another set of doctors at the other end of the hospital told us that Grandmother was doing much better.

And then suddenly, standing before us, bleary-eyed, his uniform rumpled, was Barbara's husband.

In a foolhardy, split-second decision, Giz had decided to go AWOL the minute he'd heard of his wife's condition. If a baby was about to be born, he was determined to be there, despite how the Air Force felt about it. Hitchhiking on Highway 99, he'd caught ride after ride from sympathetic drivers all too willing to stop and help a serviceman. After a dozen or so rides, he arrived in town and made his way to the hospital. Barbara was overjoyed to hear that her husband was at hand, and the beautiful, perfectly normal baby boy was born without incident.

We spent a joyous night that Christmas Eve. My father got out of bed in great spirits to begin the holiday celebrations. With our Christmas looking brighter, we turned our attention to the next problem: getting Giz back to San Francisco before the Air Force noticed he was gone. Gas was a precious commodity during the war, and none of us had enough gas coupons to last the long drive up through the valley to San Francisco. Hitchhiking slowly back on Christmas Day was his only option.

I drove Giz out to the road to begin his journey back that morning. As I made my way through the orange groves along the country road toward the main highway, the gray tule fog was so thick that I could hardly see the front end of my own car. *Oh, Lord,* I thought to myself, *how will Giz ever be able to pick up a ride in this fog? In his beige uniform, no one would be able to see him standing by the side of the road.*

But when I let him out of the car, a battered, black farm truck stopped almost immediately. Sizing up the driver as one of the local farmers out to make an early morning delivery, I felt even more discouraged. "Giz will never make it to San Francisco at this rate. I bet that fellow is just going up the road to the next ranch."

It turned out that the local farmer wasn't headed for his ranch. He was on his way up to San Francisco on business, with enough gas coupons in his wallet to take him the whole way. The farmer dropped Giz off a few blocks from the barracks. Giz slipped in with a few other fellows on their way back from Christmas services, and no one was ever the wiser about his absence from the field to attend his son's birth.

The letters from our husbands started arriving from France later that week.

SANDPAPER CHRISTMAS

R. BOB MAGART

The Christmas of my third grade, the winter of 1962, I tiptoed from my attic bed and descended the cold, squeaky staircase to steal another look at our magnificent tree. I treaded gingerly on each step because I was being bad. I'd been sent to bed, and I would be disciplined if I was caught. Our stairs led into the kitchen. Mom would be seated at her chair by the table, and by turning her head sharply, she would discover my entry.

I nudged the door open with my nose and peaked through the crack to see if the coast was clear. Mother was seated with her back partially to me, and instantly I knew that she was crying. Shame quickened in my every joint. I wanted to run to her, to hug her and drive away the tears.

I could do no such thing. For one thing, I sensed her tears were her silent cross, and I would be violating some ancient rule. For another, I wasn't supposed to be up, and such bold action would terminate my mission. So, I stealthily pushed the door forward just enough for my slight body to slip through the crack. Without making a sound, I descended the last two steps to the kitchen floor. Silently, I turned the handle and pushed the door closed.

Again, I glanced to Mother, fearful I had been discovered. No, her back was still to me. I turned to the living room arch, where a glow beckoned from the tree lights. In a flash, I was standing before the giant tree that filled from floor to ceiling almost one whole side of our living room. Around each light, the green boughs of the grand fir glistened bright and reflected off colored ornaments — red, green, blue, orange and white. Tinsel danced in reflection.

That afternoon, my mother, brother, sister and I had carefully placed the glass ornaments so they ascended in size, with the very large, glass ones on the bottom, one clear, one red, one blue, some so delicate I remembered being scolded "not to touch." We placed distinctly hardier ornaments at the fronts of boughs, where if they were bumped, they were strong and would more likely survive the fall. Near the top, Mother and my brother had attached to the very tips of the delicate branches a dozen or more tiny, gold balls, as small as the tips of my fingers. Gold was also the color of the garland that spiraled the length of the giant tree, like a road up a mountain. At the very top stood our little angel, adorned in a white robe bordered in gold, her hands in prayerful attention, and her eyes closed in concentration.

My plan now complete, I knew not what more to do. I decided to stay a few moments more, and an impish plan appeared. Next to the kitchen archway, standing on eight large legs, Mom's sideboard filled the better part of the wall. Previously playing with a cousin my age as pretend pirates or Indians, we had climbed between these cylinders. Conspiring and smart, we avoided other villains. A perfect cubbyhole was created at the end of the giant cupboard. Open space, the size of a small boy, remained before the intersect of the adjoining wall.

I slipped into this space, drew my knees up against my chest and lay my head against one of the large legs of the sideboard. In this towering world, I gazed at the magnificent tree. I was only dimly aware of the rest of the room: Mom and Dad's bedroom door, the skirted potbelly stove that sent light from small windows in its door and then, before me and through the tree branches, the front door from where Dad would soon be making his entrance.

I fell asleep, although it must have been only minutes. A cold breeze splashed me awake, and Dad was in, brushing snow from his coat and stomping his feet. He hung his green-and-black plaid coat on the hook by the stove. My hiding spot did not fail me as Dad slipped by into the kitchen. I knew to stay put. Then, I heard him discover Mother still crying.

While Dad consoled Mother, coaxing her to talk, I learned Mother's secret. She was crying because they didn't have presents for us kids. In consoling her, Father cried, too. And a warmth of joy wrapped around me because now I saw they were united. I resisted a giant urge to rush to them. With Dad, though, Mom's voice quieted. In those moments, I had learned my first inkling that there was no Santa Claus, only parents.

All was right. What was I to worry of presents when my mom and dad loved each other? It had never occurred to me that we were poor. I had never gone hungry, never gone without clothing, shelter or security. I was too young for such concerns. Father reminded Mom that the turkey for Christmas dinner was purchased and thawing on the back porch. He further reported that the rungs on the sled had been welded. *Sled*, I thought, *a sled?* He had fitted the boards tight and covered it in a single coat of paint. Tomorrow, Christmas Eve, he would coat it again and hide it under the tree that night. It would be a gift for all three of us children.

A sled, a sled. My entire frame delighted in excitement. What was I to care for another present? A sled would be great. Wrapped in the joy of Christmas coming, I was beside myself. And with this certainty, I gazed even more appreciatively on our Christmas tree. Presently, I drowsed into sleep again. When I awoke, shivering cold, the room was dark, and the tree lights were off. Mom and Dad had gone off to bed, and I was free for my escape upstairs.

***

The next morning, I woke before the others. Through the windows at both ends of the attic, dim, winter light shadowed the room in breathy coldness. My brother and sister were sound asleep across the way. But I, I was awake! Excitement and purpose thrilled me. I had a job to do; I would make a picture as a present for Mother. My sister would help me wrap it, and it would tell Mother of my undeniable love.

So many, many years later, the remainder of the day until evening is lost to my memory. We were seated at the table for dinner when our father came in, and with him was a hatless man I guessed was about fifty years old. He carried nothing. Dad announced that he was staying with us, that he would take my brother's bed, my brother would take mine, and I would sleep on the floor in my parents' bedroom. To this arrangement, Mother immediately assented. Our father simply made the announcement, our mother put another place at the table, and my brother and sister moved over on the bench to make way.

Dad had been filling the Dodge with fuel when he had discovered the man. The man was hitchhiking from Kalispell to Missoula, and some rancher had brought him to Hot Springs with the mistaken belief that he was bringing the man closer to his destination. This was true, but it had also brought him clearly off the beaten path. The man had stood by the stove at

Pehmcke's Station waiting for a ride since noon. No one was stirring. It was snowing, cold, and people were settled in for the birth of the Child. It would be nearly a thirty-mile walk to a main road, and then it was entirely possible that no one would be traveling. The man's hopes of reaching Missoula that night were drawing on impossible. Mrs. Pehmcke was closing the station and putting the man out. The man had nowhere to go but out into the cold and snow. Thus, it happened that the man joined us for Christmas.

Evening drew together. Mother made a bed for me out of blankets snug between the wall and her side of the bed. Dishes were washed, dried. We settled down. I slept soundly.

I woke to my brother and sister chattering from the living room. I burst from the bedroom. Father and Mother were seated in front of the sideboard on chairs they had brought from the kitchen. To my left, just this side of the stove, sat the stranger, also on a kitchen chair. Next, I looked to the tree, and beneath it sat my brother and sister, who hurried me to join them so presents could be opened. But, beneath the tree also sat not only a wonderful green sled but also present upon present, wrapped in colorful paper, some in newspaper comics.

I was beside myself in disbelief. Where had all these presents come from? I was dumbfounded and looked to Mother, but in the same second, I understood clearly that Santa had come. I am certain that I did not give it a second thought. Christmas had come.

***

My brother handed me my first present. It was wrapped in colorful comic strip newspaper and tied with ribbon. I opened it and found sandpaper. I looked with some disbelief to my parents who were laughing; it was intended for my father. Each present was addressed to the wrong person.

Whether it was by intuition or conspiracy, my aunt Cleo from far away Spokane, Washington, had the day before mailed us the box of presents. She and her children had gathered together an unusual assortment of presents and wrapped them, but they had addressed each to an unlikely person.

Besides the sandpaper and sled, most of that Christmas morning is lost to me, but I clearly remember one more detail of importance. It is a miniature portrait in my mind of Dad and Mom seated at the sideboard. Dad is seated to the left of Mother, his left leg crossing his right at the knee, his cup of coffee still in his right hand and his left arm hugging Mother, and Mother is laughing.

Seldom is a memory so easily recalled. It does happen, however, and most of us have early memories in which a single theme emerges brilliantly. It isn't the box of presents coming unexpectedly, although I have referred to the whole event as "my sandpaper Christmas." It isn't Father bringing home the strange man, although that remains a tender reminder of responsibility to do what we can do for those facing an emergency.

No, it happened the evening before when Dad introduced a stranger to our Christmas Eve meal, and Mother placed another plate at our table. In that act, she gave over to hospitality that which still rings across the American West.

The ease with which she agreed with Father had to have put the man at greater ease to accept. We children were provided a silent lesson of giving which no number of present giving could equal. Now that I am much older, with children of my own, I appreciate all the more Mother's acceptance of Father's judgment. It was the generosity characteristic then not to be questioned. Questioning Father would have exposed doubt not just of him but also about the goodness of all mankind. It would have hampered the Christmas spirit. Now, I know she was merely being polite to a stranger. It isn't any more complicated than that. Mom and Dad gave the man a Christmas he would not easily forget.

TO HOPE AND PRAY

CANDY CHAND

My mother was, to me, the greatest example of love, kindness, tenderness and self-sacrifice. She was the truest teacher of fairness that I have ever known, and not a day goes by that I do not miss her in my life.

I grew up in a home my parents bought just before I was born. My childhood was filled with tiny moments of caring and love—hot cocoa and cookies on a rainy afternoon, warm smiles and a pat on the back whenever I needed one. And when I grew up and moved to a house to start my own life, I didn't go far—just a few miles away. I hoped that I would be able to share my parents' love with my own children and give them the same feeling of safety and security that I'd grown up with.

But as I drove through the rain one December afternoon in 1989, all of that security seemed to be dissolving, washing away with every raindrop that fell. My mother was dying of lung cancer.

Christmas was my mother's favorite time of the year. Oh, she'd sometimes complain about the hectic season she was having, but our family tree was always carefully decorated with her prized ornaments, and I knew she took great pride in having such a special tree.

Please, God, I prayed as I drove through the rain that day, *please let my mother live through one more Christmas.* I pulled into a crowded shopping mall parking lot. *I'm not ready to let her go, and I need her here with me.* My heart was not up to shopping for presents that day, but I selected a gift or two for my husband and daughter. I knew I shouldn't let my own feelings of impending loss spoil the holiday for my young family.

In the center of an aisle stood a large display of Christmas ornaments. I thought an ornament might be a cheerful gift for my mother, something that would reconnect her with her love for Christmas and give her some hope. Once again, my thoughts took the form of prayers, and I prayed that the gift of a simple ornament would give her the hope to see this blessed day one more time. One ornament on the display stood out in particular. I was drawn to a beautiful satin and pearl-encrusted heart. I removed it from the display and walked over to the cash register, pleased with my choice. As I laid it on the counter, I turned it over. And there, outlined in seed pearls on the back of the ornament, was the word "hope."

I stared at the ornament in disbelief. This was surely a sign that my mother, too, would receive hope from my gift and was meant to survive long enough to share one more Christmas with us.

I rushed to her house with the ornament, so eager to give it to her and tell her the story that I didn't even stop to wrap it. Clutching the plastic bag to my chest, I breathlessly told her my story. I told her what hope meant to me. She smiled quietly as she listened to my tangled tale, and then she carefully hung the glimmering ornament on the big Christmas tree that stood in the corner of the living room.

But her hope was not the same as mine. As Christmas grew closer, my mother began to tell me that her desire was to die before Christmas came. She feared being ill over the holiday and forever filling our future holidays with sorrow. I assured her that all my father, my daughter and I wanted was for her to be with us for one last Christmas, sick or well. But she was insistent. "I hope to die before Christmas."

And she did. On December 7 of that year, my mother passed away, ending her long struggle against cancer. I buried the satin and pearl ornament with her. She left me, her only daughter, not only saddened but also confused.

Hadn't my prayers helped me find the "hope" ornament as a sign that she would survive, through a Christmas miracle? As the months after her death passed, I slowly began to realize that in the end, God in His wisdom had answered my mother's prayer, not mine.

THE GIFT
OF THE MAGI

APRIL KUTGER

The lawn was the color of straw. The rented house was a bland, mustard-colored ranch style on a curved street plotted out with other ranch houses with straw-colored lawns thanks to water use restrictions. A dry fall. The rolling hills that should have been turning green remained a fire danger. Less than a hundred dollars in the bank and Christmas just around the corner. Nothing new.

I was a single mother who worked in a city across a bridge, taking the train early in the morning, coming back after the winter darkness had fallen. My children were used to a few toys and *always* a book from Santa Claus, although they really knew I was the jolly old fellow. I counted on their grandmother and a few friends and coworkers to fill in the gaps.

But my mother had died only two months before. I was still grieving, crying unexpectedly, telling stories about her and listening to my children's memories, leafing through albums with pictures of her. Holding me on my christening day, putting me on the bus on my first day of school, standing beside me in my cap and gown, helping me put on my veil before my wedding, holding each of my children on their christening days.

Children are always bright-eyed on Christmas morning no matter what they get, even if it's cheap, plastic water guns and flimsy, balsa wood airplanes from a charity. One friend had bought the boys Evel Knievel action figures *with* motorcycles. A small thing, but I knew Joby and Benjie would love them. Every boy under the age of twelve loved Evel Knievel. I planned to get a baby doll for Tana. She of the pursed-lip smile and shy eyes was a little old for baby dolls, but who cares; she liked playing mother. Maybe because she hardly had one herself.

I walked up the hill from the train station. A few blocks of solitude before the onslaught of noisy children and dinner to fix. I walked slowly, head down. I knew the route by heart. Where all the cracks in the sidewalk were. How many paces until the curb. Which houses had barking dogs behind chain-link fences. I was wearing my plum wool suit and black pumps, very professional. But anyone who passed me on that evening would have thought I had gone a little crazy. I was muttering to myself. Actually, I was praying for a miracle. What kind of miracle, I didn't know. I wouldn't be getting a Christmas bonus, and I didn't expect to win any contests—hadn't entered any. No very-late-arriving tax returns. But I believed in miracles. After all, it was Christmas. My kids were shining children. God had to want to bless them.

I opened the mailbox before I went in and found the regular miscellany, including offers for car insurance and Christmas sale advertisements. A few Christmas cards. And a slim, business-sized envelope with handwriting I recognized. Someone I hadn't heard from for more than a year—my dad. We were estranged. We'd been estranged off and on for most of my life. Knowing him, it could have been a tirade of criticism. What kind of life was I living? Why didn't I go back to school? What kind of person was I? And again, why didn't I make my ex-husband support his children? Maybe if I knew where he was! The car he had given me sat unused in my driveway. A twenty-year-old gold monstrosity that feasted on gasoline and needed an alternator. Great present, Dad. I knew I'd never hear the end of that sacrificial generosity. I'd open that envelope last. Maybe I wouldn't open it at all.

Children overflowing. Hugs and stories to tell. "Wanda threw a rock at me." "I won the math quiz." "Mr. Wilson needs you to sign this." And hungry eyes. I needed a glass of wine. I needed to get out of my work clothes, especially the panty hose that left welts around my waistline and always worked their way down below my hips. God, I hated them. I washed the "lady" makeup off, ending with a splash of cold water and the whinny of a pony. I put on my nightgown, the big flannel one faded to a pink so pale that you might have thought it was white. One elbow was liberated; the fabric was so exhausted that it had just worn through. But it was comfortable, and there was certainly no man to see me looking like a frump.

On to the business of the evening. Leftover chili. No prep needed. Cornbread. Only twenty-five minutes to mix and bake. My wine. From one of the 1.5-liter bottles that cost less than five dollars. A girl has to find solace where she may. Check the homework. Make sure Joby finished all of his. Sometimes he lies. Showers. The boys shared. Had to save water. Not because there was a shortage, we just had to save on everything. Then a half hour of television. My parents had never let my sisters and me watch TV on school nights, but I needed the peace and quiet of diverted minds.

I sat on my bed and opened the mail. Bills I couldn't afford to pay until my next paycheck. A Christmas card from a friend I hadn't seen for at least ten years. It was a beautiful photograph of a perfect family dressed in matching red sweaters sitting in front of a fire, a perfectly decorated Christmas tree next to them. Was it staged? No. I knew it was their home. Why couldn't they send a card without a picture? A card from my sister with Bible text quoted. Her own message: "May you have a blessed Christmas." The "you" was underlined twice, the "blessed" three times. I guess she really meant it.

Finally, the letter from Dad. I already knew what it would be written on. Five-by-seven-inch notepaper with a crest and the exorbitant title he had carried in his final government job. Jeez. He still wore a concealed weapon under his old flight suit on the days I visited him. Talk about men who can't give up their jobs.

Dad's second wife had forced him to retire. When the war ended, she had to leave Thailand where she had lived a life of luxury, holding court for ambassadors and consulates in tuxedos and dress whites and their wives in handmade silk shantung gowns that cost a dollar. Life back in the United States on some military installation would not suit her. She'd been there and done that. For five years in the late fifties, they'd lived in officers quarters on McConnell Air Force Base in godforsaken Kansas while Dad kept the country prepared to bomb Russia.

So, what was it this time? Same paper. But, oh my God, a check! His note said, "Merry Christmas. Love, Dad." Jeez Louise. When was the last time my dad gave me money? At least ten years ago, and that was like pulling teeth. If I hadn't been close to eviction, I never would have asked him.

The check was for $500. My heart leapt. I flew into the living room. "Guess what? We got money for Christmas!"

Christmas morning wasn't overflowing. I paid off some bills with part of the money, left a hundred in my checking account. But we were as happy as newborn kittens. Tana didn't get a baby doll—she got a coveted Sasha doll with three outfits. I dressed Sasha in her pajamas and terry-cloth robe and slippers and laid her in bed next to Tana so she would see her when she woke up. "I got a Sasha doll, Mom!" I think Tana believed in Santa Claus for a minute. The boys got a football, real team football shirts and metal, cylinder storage bins with their favorite teams' symbols on them. Joby's was the Miami Dolphins, Benjie's the San Diego Chargers. Of course, each child received a book. Traditions must be carried on, or they aren't really traditions.

I had given five dollars each to Tana, Joby and Benjie to buy presents for one another. The nearby toy store had tubs in which each small toy was a dollar or less. Whistles. Plastic rings with giant rubies and diamonds. Lifelike black, plastic spiders. Yo-yos. Joby gave Tana a tiny, pink baby, the kind they put in Mardi Gras cakes; Benjie gave her a doll hairbrush. He couldn't have known the Sasha doll had long, brown hair. Tana could braid her doll's hair to match her own tangled mess. Joby received fake blood and a cricket that I knew would drive me crazy. Benjie got a compass the size of a quarter with an arrow that never stood still and a striped, wooden top. Not the greatest haul, but the givers were proud, and the receivers were truly excited and grateful.

But the best gifts on that Christmas morning were the ones I received.

My friend Ozzie had sold Tana a garage-sale wooden chair for exactly two dollars and fifty-six cents, her change after buying presents for her brothers. She knew I needed one for my sewing table, and Ozzie helped her paint it with bright yellow lacquer.

Tana was up before me on Christmas morning. Aren't all kids? She retrieved the canary chair from our neglected garage and placed it next to our popcorn-and-cranberry-strung tree. Across the chair's spindled back was a big red-and-green plaid bow that Ozzie had supplied along with the chair and paint. There were rolling-on-the-floor hugs and plenty of tears.

A few weeks before Christmas, Joby had asked me what I wanted. I said, "Oh, you don't have to give me a present."

"No, Mom, what do you really want?"

"Maybe a new spatula." Thinking bigger, I said, "Or an alternator for the car."

"Not something you need, Mom. If you could have anything, what would you ask for?"

There *was* something I really wanted. On the low side of the price range between a spatula and an alternator. "I'd like a clock radio." I wanted to be able to wake up to music instead of a blasted buzzer.

That was the end of the conversation.

On Christmas morning, Joby handed me a haphazardly wrapped box large enough to hold a cowboy hat. I held it to my ear and gently shook it. Something knocked around inside.

"Don't shake it, Mom," he cried.

Dark-eyed Joby was bouncing with delight before I even opened the box. Inside was his own clock radio. Scuffed up a little, some fingerprints, a smudge that looked like tar, but

I knew it worked. My mother had given it to him the year before. I started to blubber. For my mother and for my little O'Henry son.

But that wasn't the end of it.

Seven-and-a-half-year-old Benjie handed me a card in a white envelope with "Mom" written on the front. "This is my present for you, Mom." He stepped back and smiled tentatively. I noticed that his ringleted head was badly in need of a haircut.

I pulled out a blue Hallmark sympathy card with a picture of a dove.

On the front, the flourishing script read, "We are thinking of you with deepest sympathy. Those we love are with the Lord and He has promised to be with us. If they are with Him and He is with us . . . they cannot be far away."

Inside: "Though our words of understanding are inadequate and few, our hearts are filled with loving thoughts and sympathy for you."

Then Benjie's penciled closing:
"Love Benjie
and Merry C—
hrismas."

***

Now my Christmas dinners are made for seventeen; my children and their spouses have given me nine wild grandsons and a princess of a granddaughter. Telling the story of the year of the chair, the clock radio and the card of sympathy has become a Christmas tradition, along with a book for everyone on Christmas morning. The Christmas miracle I had prayed for as I walked home from the train in that dry, winter twilight did not come in the form of a $500 check from my father. My Christmas miracle was found in the kind and generous hearts of my shining children who knew that Christmas was not about what they received but about what they gave.

HOMELESS
SANTA

JENNIFER BASYE SANDER

A crummy 1988 was winding down as my roommate, Margaret, and I set out for an afternoon snack on Christmas Eve. I'd just returned to California after a dark three months of hiding in the Swedish woods in my own private Ingmar Bergman film after a star-crossed romance. My arrival home had been as dramatic as my sudden departure some months before. I was booked on a Pan Am flight from London to San Francisco. Having been away from home for so long, I told myself that if I missed the flight, I would take the next available one to the United States, Pan Am 103. I made my flight with just minutes to spare. Passengers for the San Francisco flight were checking in at a counter directly across from the New York flight, and I absentmindedly joined the New York line. When I noticed my mistake, I joked about it with the folks near me in that line and made my way across the room to the other flight counter.

As my parents drove me home from the airport over slow-moving California freeways, they told me about the midair explosion of Flight 103 over Lockerbie, Scotland. "But I saw those people," I said. "How can they all be dead?" My dreams that night were haunted by the image of the Scottish countryside strewn with carefully packed Christmas gifts, steamed puddings from Harrods and little piles of the Christmas candy that an airport Santa had handed to everyone waiting in the security line.

When I woke on Christmas Eve morning, yes, I was back home, but it was a strange sensation. I felt tentative, oddly disconnected from what was going on around me. I'd come home after an absence of months, but I didn't feel like I'd come home in one piece.

Craving the taste of authentic Mexican food after so much Swedish butter and cream, Margaret and I chose to head for a ramshackle burrito house in a dicey part of town. Near the train tracks and several homeless shelters, it was not the part of town you'd expect to find two middle-class girls on Christmas Eve. We ordered our burritos and sat outside in the sun to wait for our order. The streets around us were deserted; office workers and commuters had gone home to get an early start on the holiday.

Margaret nudged my arm. "Oh, great," she said. "Looks like we're about to get hit up for money." A disheveled man was making his way toward us across the parking lot, his progress slowed both by his age and by the oversized, green sack he carried on his back. His hair was long and snowy white, his thick beard spread over the top of his tattered jacket. Margaret and I clucked our tongues and shook our heads and began to search our pockets for loose change to disperse him quickly and get on with our meal.

Slowly and quietly, he made his way across the blacktop until he was standing in front of us. He stopped, and without saying a word, he rolled his heavy bag off his shoulder and set it on the ground. Untying the top, he reached in and began to rummage through the contents of his bag. Margaret and I watched quietly as he found what he was seeking and removed his hand. He held a shiny, red apple. With great dignity, he held it out to Margaret. She accepted his gift.

He reached into his duffel bag a second time and this time pulled out a candy bar and offered it to me. "No," I said. "We can't take your food. You need it!" She and I both held our gifts back out to him. "We can't take your food."

The man smiled shyly and shook his head. "I can't eat it," he said sadly. "My teeth are no good. Merry Christmas."

He would not accept the money we tried to give him that afternoon; he just kept quietly shaking his head and smiling as we tried to press dollar bills into his hand. Finally, he agreed to the purchase of a cup of coffee. He took the steaming foam cup and, shouldering his bag once again, continued on his way.

I have told this story many times since it happened, and every time I shake my head. I think about the quiet man with the big, white beard and the bag of presents who gave two privileged girls part of the only food he had. It would have been so easy for us to get up and move inside of the café that day, avoiding someone who looked scary. I am so thankful that we stayed where we were, sitting on the porch fence, open to what life could teach us. The burrito house has long since been torn down, but every time I drive past the spot, I give silent thanks to the man with the generous heart. He reminds me that we should all give openly and often to everyone we meet, every chance we get, 365 days of the year.

About the Contributors

JENNIFER ALDRICH

Since the first time she slipped on her grandmother's high-heeled shoes and I. Magnin jacket, Jennifer Aldrich has imagined herself into dozens of rich fantasy lives. A hopeless Anglophile, she regularly attends fancy dress parties and takes tea at four o'clock daily. She lives in Northern California with her husband, another hopeless Anglophile, and their son, whom they are raising imaginatively.

ELAINE AMBROSE

Elaine is the co-author of *Menopause Sucks* and *Drinking with Dead Women Writers.* Her short stories and feature articles appear in several anthologies and magazines; and she owns Mill Park Publishing. She organizes Write by the River writers' retreats in Idaho and creates a sassy blog called *Midlife Cabernet*. Find more details at www.ElaineAmbrose.com.

DEE AMBROSE-STAHL

Dee has been writing since she was a small child. She still resides in her hometown and teaches English at the middle school she attended. She has served as both reviewer and contributor for Holt, Rinehart and Winston. Her fiction and photography have appeared in specialty corgi magazines. When not writing and teaching, she enjoys breeding, raising and showing Pembroke Welsh corgis.

RUTH ANDREW

Ruth is a freelance writer living in Spokane, Washington. Her previous short stories and articles have appeared in newspapers, lifestyle magazines and anthologies, including *My Mom Is My Hero* and *My Dog Is My Hero*. She is working on her first novel. You may read more about her at www.ruthandrew.com and beeconcise.wordpress.com.

JO ANNE BOULGER

Jo Anne Boulger resides in Pebble Beach, California, where she keeps busy with various volunteer endeavors, painting and writing. She is a widow with four children and eleven grandchildren, and a first great-grandchild due in December of 2012.

RUTH CAMPBELL BREMER

Ruth is a freelance writer, blogger and aspiring novelist. Her stupefying brilliance can be found at www.insightfulish.com.

DAVID SCOTT CHAMBERLAIN

David has a communications degree from University of Southern California, masters in communication from California State University at Los Angeles, masters in educational multimedia from the Univerisy of Arizona, and works for NetApp. His mother Barbara has begun a series of mysteries set in Carmel—the first is *A Slice of Carmel*. She is currently the president of Northern California Pen Women, and she enjoys writing, storytelling and giving seminars on creative writing and storytelling.

CANDY CHAND

Candy has authored seven books. She lives in Northern California and can be reached at PatCan85@hotmail.com.

HARRY FREIERMUTH

Rev. Harry Freiermuth is a member of the Central Coast Writers branch of California Writers Club, who specializes in short stories and has written a historical fiction novel. He is a retired Roman Catholic priest of the diocese of Monterey in California.

KATHLEEN (KM) GALLAGHER

KM is a writer, entrepreneur and pet travel specialist. She is the author of *SoleMate: The Runner's Companion for Taking Life in Stride*. Currently she is working on a series of winery guidebooks, *Sip + Slobber: A Dog's Companion to California's Dog Friendly Whineries*. KM also serves as president of StoryBiz, a content strategy firm that uses storytelling to build brands. She holds undergraduate degrees in history and philosophy and a masters in business administration from Northeastern University Graduate School of Business. KM, along with her dogs, splits her time between Texas and California.

JEANNE GILPATRICK

Jeanne lives in Oakland, California, with her dog Charlie. She won a twenty-five-word essay contest at age twelve and has been writing ever since. She recently completed a young adult novel and is sharpening her pencils in anticipation of retirement. You can reach Jeanne at: jeannejo2@att.net.

PAT HANSON

Pat Hanson, Ph.D., is a veteran health educator, writer and public speaker living in Monterey, California. She lectures nationally on aging positively, and is a columnist for the magazine *Crone: Women Coming of Age* (www.cronemagazine.com). Visit her website at www.invisiblegrandparent.com.

BJ HOLLACE

BJ is a published author, editor and speaker who takes the ordinary and turns it into an extraordinary story. Her passion as a writer is to touch the hearts of her readers and empower them to follow their own dreams. Currently, she is working on a novel series and coaching first-time authors.

ROSI HOLLINBECK

Rosi specializes in children's writing. Her work has been featured in issues of *High Five, Highlights,* and *Stories for Children* magazines, and her children's short story, *Helen's Home Run,* won first place in the 2011 Foster City International Writer's Contest, Children's Division. Her middle-grade novel, *The Incredible Journey of Freddy J.* was a finalist in the Grace Notes Publishing Discovering the Undiscovered contest. She also has a story-poem that will be included in the 2012 British anthology *Fifty Funny Poems for Children.* She regularly writes reviews for the *Sacramento Book Review;* and her blog, rosihollinbeckthewritestuff.blogspot.com, has nearly a thousand readers a month.

PAUL KARRER

Paul has been published in the *San Francisco Chronicle, Christian Science Monitor, Education Week, Teacher Magazine,* and interviewed on NPR. His essay "A Letter to My President, The One I Voted For," went viral. He is a fifth-grade teacher and union negotiator in Castroville, California.

JULAINA KLEIST-CORWIN

Julaina is the Creative Writing Instructor for the City of Dublin, California. She has won first place awards in short story contests and been published in several anthologies by the San Francisco Writers Conference and Las Positas College. She is a field supervisor for intern teachers. You can find her blogging at timetowritenow.blogspot.com, or her website julaina.homestead.com. Her son Adrian Toryfter, was an audio designer for Diablo Valley College theater, where he had a fatal accident backstage.

APRIL KUTGER

April is an award-winning author of fiction and nonfiction. When she's not writing, April volunteers as a basic skills tutor and swims on a masters team. Christmas Eve with her three children and ten grandchildren is her favorite day of the year.

LIZA LONG

Liza is a teacher, writer, musician and single mother of four (mostly) delightful children. She bought her 1925 Model M Steinway grand piano at a thrift store. Her anthology *Little White Dress: Women Explore the Myth and Meaning of Wedding Dresses* won a 2012 Bronze Ippy Award in Women's Issues. She blogs at www.anarchistsoccermom.com.

INGRID E. LUNDQUIST

Ingrid is founder of the Book-in-Hand Roadshow and author of the *Dictionary of Publishing Terms: Words Every Writer Needs to Know.*

After an international award-winning career as an event designer/producer, she rediscovered her first love—writing and art. She is owner of TLC Publishing, an imprint of The Lundquist Company, her event firm. She writes articles for event industry publications and is author of *Results-Driven Event Planning: Using Marketing Tools to Boost Your Bottom Line.* She travels on a whim and is an accomplished photojournalist. See www.TheBookInHandRoadshow.com and www.FiveWeeksInFlorence.com and www.ingridlundquist.com.

R. BOB MAGART

R. Bob Magart is a freelance writer, a former businessman and a father of five. He makes his home between Montana and Washington and is an avid outdoorsman and cyclist. He was born on Christmas Day, 1952.

LAURA MARTIN

Laura is a freelance writer and photographer whose work has appeared in *Sacramento* magazine, *Solano* magazine, *Via* magazine, the *San Jose Mercury News,* the *Boston Globe,* the *San Francisco Chronicle, Susurrus,* and other publications throughout Northern California. She is an Amherst Writers and Artists affiliate and leads writing workshops throughout Sacramento. "A Sears Catalog Christmas" is part of a working collection of creative nonfiction stories, entitled *The Last Night on Jackson Street,* about growing up in the small sawmill town of Weed, California.

VALERIE REYNOSO PIOTROWSKI

Valerie is an award-winning writer, poet and fundraiser. She and her husband, John Piotrowski, reside in El Dorado Hills, California, with their three beloved dogs, and are active in philanthropic support of a number of community and charitable causes. They own a high-end spa franchise, Elements Therapeutic Massage Studio, in Folsom, California.

LOUISE REARDON

Louise is a fourth-generation Californian from the Central Valley, a mother, a wife and a teacher. After teaching for fifty years and volunteering almost as long for causes like food banks and equal housing, Louise is now enjoying her senior years.

CHERYL RIVENESS

"Living on an island in the Pacific Northwest is a writer's dream," Cheryl says. "It's a wonderful creative environment. Although I have lived in many places, my heart has always been here." You can follow Cheryl at www.theislandposts.com.

JENNIFER BASYE SANDER

Jennifer is a *New York Times* bestselling author, former Random House senior editor and the mother of two amazing sons. She teaches publishing skills and nonfiction writing, and runs writing retreats in Lake Tahoe and on her great-grandfather's farm in Washington state. Learn more about her retreats at www.writebythelake.com or www.writeatthefarm.com.

JACK SKILLICORN

Jack was born in 1933 in Watsonville, California, where he grew up, worked and attended Monterey Peninsula College. He studied, played football, dropped out and joined the USAF. He served during the Korean conflict for four years, then returned to the USAF during the Vietnam conflict, after which he returned to college for a bachelor degree in accounting. Jack was first published in the *California County*, Journal of the County Supervisors Association of California with an article called "Who Said You Could Run a County Like a Business?" In retirement he began writing stories for grandchildren and family.